I0462501

COPYRIGHT © 2019

By ROBERT HARINGTON & MARIUS BRADLEY

Table of Contents

ABOUT THE BOOK

This book will show you how to stop procrastination and get organized now. There is a fact that we all have to face in an effort to get organized: to be successful at getting organized, we have to be in the right place mentally and emotionally to take action. Without the correct mindset and emotional supports, the approach and the work of organizing our space or life can bring on the same sense of being overwhelmed that occurs in child rearing, managing our finances, or in juggling relationships, jobs and families. Our success depends on changing our mindset in order to change our life. So to put a band-aid on the dread of being overwhelmed, this book has provided ideas and solutions to permanently cure procreastination and laziness. By doing this we convince ourselves that we are moving forward on our goal to get organized. We are taking action, but our habits and attitudes are leading us to take actions that are not helpful and may even be the wrong things necessary to achieve our goal. Our primary success is a form of controlled procrastination. Geting information from this book about ways to Get Organized can be great fun. It can also be an interesting, even an entertaining means of finding information about organizing one's home, office or life. We are convinced that the task before us requires us to gather just a little more information on the subject, then we can take action.

The truth is that, this book will help you find numerous step-by-step processes and lists of tips on methods you can use to cure procrastination and get organized. The question we still face is, where do we find the help to get us mentally and emotionally prepared to take action and follow through with our goals? How do we stop procrastinating and get beyond our paralysis from the analysis?

For a growing number of people, the answer to that question has come in the form of positive affirmation programs. These powerful and easy to use book, delivers habit control and emotion/behavior modification tools. Your success with this book will help you end the terrible cycle of delay and failure you have experienced in your efforts to get your space or your life, organized. Wouldn't you love to develop the mindset and emotional support needed to take action and be able to say, I Am Organized Now?

INTRODUCTION

Curing Procrastination is related to the task of overpowering fear. If an individual becomes successful in conquering the fears that lead to the delaying of vital projects then, the possibility of curing of procrastination is very high. To cure procrastination is not always related to exercising self-discipline or perhaps vehemently making headway towards the objectives, but in fact, it is to be aware basically of the causes of procrastination. For any individual to cure procrastination, it is very essential to first determine the rational reasons for the fears and then, find ways to confront the fears, so as to progress in life. Most of the people are afraid of 2 things: Failures and Success. Curing Procrastination becomes easier after determining these 2 parameters that cause an individual to procrastinate.

We've all been there. You've been given 30 days to prepare for a paper-yet you do not even start on the paper until the day before its due. This is called Procrastination. A wise man described procrastination as the "dream killer" because it destroys productivity. Let's define procrastination:

Procrastination: the act of procrastinating; putting off or delaying or deferring an action to a later time.

This is simply one meaning of procrastination.

There are many other meanings and interpretations but for the sake of simplicity, we will just use the above definition. How many of us "putt off" until tomorrow what we should be doing today? It is believed that the majority of Americans procrastinate on a high scale every day. Whenever we practice procrastination it destroys our productivity- killing our dreams. Just think for a minute: what can you possibly accomplish (that's worth accomplishing) if you fail to take action? If you put off cleaning your home you will eventually be living in a pig pin, not to mention the health issues that can arise from poor maintenance. Another version defines procrastination as "intentionally and habitually putting off what should be done." Notice that procrastination is intentional. So many people fool themselves into believing that procrastination is something that just "happens" without any human effort or contribution. This, however, is not true. You have to actively participate in order to procrastinate. When you know something needs to be done and you choose not to do it, you are actively involved in causing your own failure. Imagine if you felt that your body was just not functioning properly and you made plans to go to the doctor. Your appointment arrives and because you felt like you worked hard all week and you deserved a little rest, you put it off. One day turns into one week, one week into a month, and finally, you just forget about going at all. After passing out at work, you find that you have a condition that could have been prevented if you would have done it. Do not let procrastination kill your dreams of being a success. There is no miracle solution for procrastination except to take action. Taking the necessary action when required to be the only solution for procrastination. Most people procrastinate when it's time to go to the gym or work out but report feeling better going to the gym or exercising. Whenever you procrastinate, you are left feeling guilty and even depressed at times. People who lack the motivation to achieve even minimal tasks have been found to be borderline depressed or manically depressed. You will always feel better after you get things done.Procrastination adds to depression and can cause one to experience bad health, bad relationships, failing grades, and poor work performance which can lead to the loss of one's employment. No one wants to experience these things happening to them, so why do they procrastinate?

Recognizing Procrastination

The first step in overcoming procrastination is acknowledging that procrastination exists. You can not get to "victory" until you first recognize that you have a problem. It's kind of like having a medical issue. You can not get the treatment that is required until you first acknowledge and diagnose the problem, then you can move on to the problem.

Establish "why" you procrastinate

Understanding the "why" behind your procrastination moves you closer to overcoming it. Let's say you are putting off cleaning your house. Maybe it's because you've allowed it to get so out of hand that it's overwhelming to you and you just wish it would go away. Usually, procrastination takes place whenever a task that needs to be done is not pleasurable. Most humans have no problem with getting things done that's pleasurable to them. Its human nature. We are designed to move away from pain and draw close to pleasure.

CHAPTER ONE

The Roots Of Procrastination

The difference between the winner and the loser is in their daily habits because your future is buried in your daily routines. Habits - they predict and determine your future. One of these habits that can mar your future is procrastination.

Procrastination is the habit of delaying action or avoiding an essential activity until a later time. It is the tendency to wait for a perfect condition before taking action. But sadly, a perfect condition may not come thus, you won't get anything done. This habit, if not terminated, will damage and hinder your career advancement, damage your relationship and health, prevents you from achieving what you really want in life and eventually make you feel unhappy and unfulfilled. Slack habits are as bad as vandalism!

According to the law of "cause and effect", procrastination can look at and be visualized as the effect of some causes which I termed the roots of procrastination. Invariably, it's these roots, the causes, that unconsciously provide the necessary nourishment for procrastination. Incredibly, most of us that procrastinate have not been able to identify these causes and it's therefore difficult for us to overcome it despite our struggle to live without procrastinating. Nevertheless, being a chronic procrastinator before, I will unveil some of the roots of procrastination and how to eradicate them. Read on!

1. Ignorance and Lack of Preparation

"Ignorance is a disease," they say and opportunity meet the prepared mind. One of the symptoms of this disease is procrastination. Ignorance is the absence of right information that could help you harness an idea. Because you lack information, ill-informed, ignorant or unprepared you don't know how to go about executing and managing the brilliant ideas that come into your mind. You can't write the business proposal, start your own business, and so on. The excuse is that I'm not prepared. Try to have a self retrospect into all the opportunities you have put off if any is as a result of lack of preparation or lack of information. If there is any, then ask yourself this question: when am I going to be prepared and better be informed?

To eradicate ignorance and lack of preparation, you have to seek for more information. I once decided to execute an idea that I got. It's all about how to solve a problem facing some individuals and organizations. But I knew nothing about how to go about it. And I never get started. The truth is that if you don't have the information, you won't be interested, and as a result, you can't be involved and eventually, no action will be taken.

To get information, read magazines, books, internal reports, talk to people who you think are incline in the area of your idea and also do research. Get yourself familiar with what you need. Familiarity often leads to interest.

2. Fear

Fear is trembling before that which confront you. And because you trembled you avoid confronting that which confront you. Every one of us is being confronted with ideas and opportunities every day; that is well utilized and acted upon will make us stand out and let our name enter the profile of successful people in our generation. To some of us, it's the fear of failure, probably because we have failed before. Failure doesn't mean you are inferior, you are wasting your time or you will never make it; it only creates an avenue for you to demonstrate your superiority, learn something new, and do it in a more brilliant way as you start afresh.

How many times have you avoided or delayed doing something because of fear? Fear of making mistakes? Fear of failing? Name them! It was Alan Lakein who said that "fear is the root of all avoidance". I have discovered that nothing can't cripple a man more than fear because even the physically crippled can be medically manipulated with artificial legs to drive a car, but a complete fearful man with two legs may not be a passenger thus, will not change his position.

To overcome fear, you must:

i.) Identify the cause of your fears;

ii.) Learn from your past experiences;

iii.) Develop boldness and confront your fears;

iv.) Try, start, begin doing what you fear and what you fear will start to disappear; later or sooner the fears will be no more.

3. Distraction

Distractions are unexpected interruption that makes additional and annoying demands on your time. They are to sidetrack you and make you lose concentration and shift your focus from what you are actually doing. A lot of distractions can make you procrastinate an important task. Most of us that procrastinate is often in most cases easily distracted. Most of these things that distract us are sometimes our daily routines such as watching television, listening to a conversation in the next office, wondering who just walk down the staircase and so on. Just make a list of those things that easily distract you. And think if any of these things have actually made you procrastinate.

To avoid being distracted, you must:

i.) Plan what you want to do every day with a written purpose of why you want to do these things prior to the beginning of the day. Planning leads directly to action.

ii.) Keep the TO DO LIST in front of you or have it in mind. Keeping it in front of you gives you a choice of what to do next.

iii.) Remove every potential distracting stimulus from around you or avoid them.

iv.) Ask yourself what is the best use of my time now. This will keep you focused and definitely increase your concentration on what you are supposed to do in your TO DO LIST.

"Any problem that its causes are known is half solved".Procrastination is not an exception. Lack of preparation and information, fear, and distractions are the most common reasons why people procrastinate. These factors make the subject to always find one reason or the other never to act or take a decision. However, commitment and dedication of oneself to the solutions proffered to each of these causes is undoubtedly believed to bring success to you in your attempt to overcoming procrastination.

Procrastination disorder is hard to deal with if you are not aware that you have one in the first place. After all, it has become part of your life. You can identify the symptom right away when you look at the way you handle your important task.

Let say, right now you strongly want to stop procrastinating. You swear to yourself that you'll start doing your important task in the next 5 minutes. The 5 minutes is gone. The task is already sitting in front of you. You are ready to start.

However, for some unknown reason, in a split second, you choose to do something else instead of starting your task. You cannot explain what's happening and you enjoy doing something else instead of doing what you are supposed to do. You'll also justify with yourself why you should continue what you are doing and you'll also start telling yourself that you can always start and finish your more important task later on.

If this is what happens to you most of the time, then it's very likely you have a procrastination disorder. This article will not elaborate further on the other symptoms but will focus more on how you can deal with this self-destructive pattern.

Following are some of the symptoms

- When you want to avoid some task which you consider as unpleasant then you replace that task with some less important task like while filling the tax form, suddenly you realize that your desk is dirty. Immediately your focus will be shifted to cleaning the desk but again where is the mop? Now you will go and find the mop. While finding the mop you may come across some other left behind the task and this goes on for eternity.

- When it is time to act on your particular idea you pause and think that let us wait some more time.
- You think that you know very less about your idea, so you need to do more research before acting on it.
- Find some fault in you. For example, you want to find a life partner but you find some fault in you and think that with this fault it is not possible to find a good partner.
- Constantly remembering the past. Whenever some task called for an action you will stop and think that in past you fail in similar circumstances.

Stages Of Procrastinators Syndrome

Stage 1

- It will make you lazy. The more comfortable you get then the less you will want to do. It will get harder to make yourself do anything if something is not done about it sooner than later. You will not want to escape because there will always be an excuse to prevent it from happening.
- Make excuses. These are easy to come by for most people. They have heard these since they were old enough to understand. Parents use them, family, friends, coworkers, and other people have some stored for future use when needed. Stockpiling would be the correct terminology to use.

Stage 2

We are all to familiar with the terms below because we have used them at some point during our life. They seem to be the first thing that pops into our mind to be said.

- No, I will not. This is used in reference to doing something. If you do not want to do it then you freely tell someone that you will not do it. The issue is not up for debate. It will not happen.
- I can not do it. This is one of the most used and one of the easiest to use. Say it right now to see how easy it flows right off the end of your tongue. When something gets hard or confusing the first comment that is said, "I can not do that." We think it excuses us from doing something but in reality, it only puts it off until later.
- I want. This is as straight forward as anyone can get when they are not going to do something. Think about how often and how many times you use this phrase in a day?
- I do not want to. This is used a lot to get out of doing something. But most of the time the other person has heard it so much that it does not work anymore.
- Do I have to? If only I had a penny every time I heard that comment I would be a millionaire. Hey, wait a minute! If I had a penny for every time that I have used it then that would make me a double millionaire.
- I am busy and I have got something else to do. Ah yes, what a turnaround. Someone needs your help or assistance and you do not have time or do not want to help. I have heard this several times but when the tables are turned it does not work as well.

Stage 3

Get up, get out, and get going. That is the simple solution to get results. Stop wasting time and start using time wisely.

- Run an interference. When all else fails and you want to overcome the three stages of procrastinators syndrome then run interference so that you will always be on your toes and at the top of your game. This will not allow anything to get through to interfere with your recovery.
- Have a destination. One important point to remember is to always know where you are going. Do not put things in automatic mode. This can lead to trouble. Have full control at all times.

There might be a remote possibility that you have found yourself, will find yourself or might be in this situation right now. You are infected with the procrastinator's syndrome and need a cure. The above should help remedy the problem.

Here's how you might overcome your procrastination problem within just five easy steps

Step 1:-Admit that you are living in a destructive pattern. It is vital, because, without an awareness that you have a chronic procrastination problem, you'll not do something to cure it. It will be vitally essential that you pay close attention to your procrastination pattern because you want to know how you can interrupt this pattern with the next steps. Different people have different procrastination pattern.

Step 2:-Ask yourself why you procrastinate. After observing your own procrastination pattern, then start looking for reasons why you procrastinate. Is the task too difficult or too big? Are you feeling overwhelmed? Are you scared that you might fail? The key reason why this step is very important is to understand further the psychological reasons that trigger you to procrastinate and consequently come out with a cure for each reason.

Step 3:-List down the cures for each reason. You will want to do this in order to know what to do when you face the same reason in the future. Let say your reason for procrastinating is because you feel overwhelmed. The cure, for this reason, will be to break a big task to smaller tasks and work in blocks of time. The different reason has a different cure and you might want to brainstorm for the cures. There are many resources you can use to come out with a working cure for any of your reasons.

Step 4:-Start applying your cure. Specifically, you might want to start with the existing important task that you have been procrastinating for a very long time. You already know the reasons and the cures and now it's time to apply it. Consequently, you will get started with that important task.

Step 5:-Repeat, repeat and repeat. Whenever you are about to procrastinate, alert yourself that you are about to go into a destructive pattern. Remind yourself about the steps above. The process is going to be much faster this time because you already know your pattern, your reasons, your cures and what to do in that situation. As you repeat the same process again and again, you'll develop a new productive pattern and consequently free yourself from procrastination.

Types of Procrastination

- **Skill deficits:-**The first type of procrastination is the skill deficit. When you lack the skill and that element in you that could help your project or idea, you procrastinate. One good way to stop procrastinating in skill deficits is by starting easy or simply quitting the project and working on something you are skilled at.

- **External obstacles:-**This is when you are disturbed or in a situation where you think this is not the perfect time to start. "The perfect time to start" isn't really an obstacle because the right time is almost always in hand. Perfect time to start is about you being in alignment with yourself and your surroundings. A disturbed brain procrastinate.

- **Emotional problems:-**Depression, lack of confidence or even excessive emotional stress are some of the basic reasons you might be procrastinating. This type of procrastination happens because even though you have all the qualities and resources, you are quite helpless about taking real solid action about completing your tasks.

- **Addictive escapism:-**Some people out there are always searching for a way to act upon things they want to quit by trying to find solutions to their problems. Their problem is that they keep searching for an answer to their problem that they want to avoid acting upon.

Unrecognized inner truth:

-This reason actually relates to me. Some of us have this understanding that we are not meant to do this. No matter how persuaded or motivated we look from the outside, from the inside we have this calling that the path we are upon is not that we are supposed to walk upon. Your inner voice is making you procrastinate.

It is important to know why you are procrastinating to actually beat it. Whenever you feel you are procrastinating make sure you categorize it and move forward by taking the most appropriate action that is

Statistics On Procrastination

Statistics on procrastination basically involves the usage of statistics, normally utilized in organizations for gathering information on the number of procrastinating workers. This would help the organization to find the causes affecting their profits and the reasons, as to why workers procrastinate. It is already well known that procrastination is a term, which makes the person defer a task for a later period, which was mostly supposed to be performed at a current period. There are many reasons as to why people prefer to avoid them. This would be of help only when good statistics on procrastination is at hand.

Although a person can indulge in procrastination at any point in time, there are high probabilities of occurrence of procrastination at the approach of a deadline. More so, procrastination can also occur during odd moments also. On some occasions, it may also happen that even before a person comes to know of the reason, he would become a victim of procrastination.

Help from the Medical Fraternity:

Possible help for studying statistics on procrastination could come from the medical fraternity. This would happen only when people would find relevant information on the causes and then, rectify the problem. Thanks to the proper statistics on procrastination, a person would receive valuable help in understanding the numerous reasons as to why a person gets into the procrastinating trap. In addition, it would also help in knowing as to whether there are some effective ways of treating the problem or not.

With the availability of proper statistics on procrastination, there would be a possibility of deeply analyzing the findings and learning the best methods for curing the problem. In such situations, those people who are interested to know the statistics on procrastination could have a check on places as the Procrastination Research Group and other such papers, which are related to the procrastination study, in which many useful statistics on procrastination can be included.

Rough Estimations:

Based on some figures, it is estimated that as much as 95 % of the people are prone to procrastination. Amongst them, 20 % of them are chronic procrastinators. These people have an increased chance of losing their jobs, have financial problems and have serious problems with their relationship with others.

In addition, when experts do have statistics on procrastination at hand, they can formulate theories as to why a person embarks on procrastination in the initial stage. Although, it is known that anxiety is the leading cause as to why people procrastinate, there are high chances of finding other reasons behind procrastination, which would highlight the problem. It is essential to have a serious think on procrastination, as it affects both the individual and the organization where he works.

Even for the best of us, there are days when nothing gets done. A big problem most of us face when it comes to doing things, starting something, continuing or finishing something is procrastination.

It is important to realize that the solutions for procrastination are often very simple. (That's a problem for most of us). It involves you making a conscious decision to go ahead and do the task.

When you look for tips on procrastination, you will find that they all say the same thing - " Act now!" No matter how difficult something looks, it will not become doable until you have tried to do it. Every achiever says the same thing, it comes to just going ahead with action and doing something rather than just thinking about it.If you have been finding yourself at the receiving end time and time again, unable to reach your goals this is for you.

It is time to stop being a procrastinator.

Unless you are able to have a clear decision, you cannot get ahead and act. The best decisions often are made quickly. Almost on the spur of the moment. Haven't you heard the saying "strike while the iron is hot"? That is always the key. If you wait to think and second guess yourself. I guarantee you, every time, you will always be stuck in the same boat always. You'll do next to nothing.

There is no growth in life without a conscious decision to act.

For many people the biggest reason they cannot stop being a procrastinator is the fact that they are overcome and overwhelmed by their fears. Consider how these fears come into being in the first place. Fear is a small seed of doubt that grows as you think of it repeatedly. If you want to be able to stop procrastinating you have to kill that flame. The best way to do this is to not feed the fear with other doubtful thoughts. Kill the thought by acting. Once you act on your decision, your fears will fade. Every single person that has found ways to overcome procrastination talks about how they found the strength for it within themselves. Prioritizing on what you need to do is the first step. Staying focused on a task comes from an inner resolve and the only person standing in the way of completing a task, are you? Once you realize this, it gets very easy to do everything you set out to do. You will be able to easily achieve all your dreams and ambitions the day you decide to stop being a procrastinator. The secret acts on your hunches, guts reactions, flashes of inspiration. They will be your own solutions to you not being a procrastinator anymore....

How to Overcome Laziness

Laziness can easily pervade your life if you are not careful. It will strike when you have an important task or project that you need to get done but there is a voice in your head saying just sit on the couch for a little bit longer and before you know it the whole day is gone. Laziness is a state learned helplessness in which you simply ignore the thing that you should do even though you have the ability to accomplish them.

The first thing to do is to deal with that little voice inside your head that is standing in the way of you getting something done and telling you no. The thing to understand is that this is nothing more than a mental state and that it can be altered when you decide to do so. A trick that I like to use to break free of this is to force myself to start on the project I am working on by doing the simplest aspect of it first. This gets me into a rhythm and helps me recognize that the work wasn't as bad as I had originally thought it was.

Another way to conquer laziness is to get in tune with the fluctuations of your energy levels throughout the day. Often time you will feel tired at some point in the day which only fuels your lazy feelings. The problem is that most of the time you are not really tired. Some quick exercise can get the blood flowing in your body and provide you with the energy boost to get going.

Knowing why you have to complete the task ahead of you is important. Sometimes you lose sight of the overall goal that you are working on when you get bogged down in the individual steps of the process. Trying to lose weight can be difficult because some days you don't want to work out even though you really do want to accomplish your overall goal of losing weight. Start to think of what you want to get done and realize that these small steps will get you where you want to go.

Most of us have more than one task to accomplish in the span of a day and the indecisiveness of what to start working on first can prolong your procrastination and laziness. Choosing one thing to work on at a time will give you the focus you need to work straight through on that task and put everything else on the back burner until it is time for you to move on.

Working for too long can burn you out and hinder your creativity. In order to stop being lazy sometimes it is necessary to take a break or reward yourself for the work you have already put in. Getting in the habit of rewarding yourself after your work gives you something to look forward to and changes the state of your mind where you can just relax and not worry about the tasks you must do.

Overcoming laziness means that you are going to have to sometimes just force yourself to do the task that you don't want to do. You come to find that the thing you dread the most isn't always as bad as you had it cracked up to be. It can be beneficial that you simply act and not think about what you have to do. Once you get going laziness seems to fade away rather quickly.

Tips to Beat Laziness

Laziness makes that before certain activities that you have to perform in your day to day, your body feels bad, without energy, demotivated, and do not perform these tasks that you know would make a difference in your life.

Laziness causes your attention to dissolving with any other activity that passes in front of you. Eliminating or dissolving from your mind the main objective for which you want to fight, moving away from your real objectives, your true success, and development.

There are 4 types of Sloth

- Physical laziness
- Mental laziness
- Existential laziness
- Spiritual laziness

Whatever your type of laziness, will take you to poverty and poverty if you do not put a stop as soon as possible. In Proverbs 6 of verse 6-11, the Bible tells us of a close relationship of misery and poverty with laziness. They are friends that when they come together, they are inseparable.

Tell me, do you want to be poor all your life? Then keep in mind the following tips that I will give you to combat laziness:

1. Check your physiological signals

- Maybe your laziness is due to:
- Excess of physical activity.
- Lack of sleep.
- Bad eating habits.
- Lead a life too sedentary.

2. Check your reasons

Feel better, have more free time or financial independence, feel comfortable with yourself, overcome a personal challenge ... or simply, because you like it. Nothing motivates as much as being clear about why you are going to do a task.

3. Do simple things first.

Start with the task you most want to do, in order to fight laziness effectively. The tip of victory is to start with the simplest things to do, which will break your inner resistance

4. Divide and Conquer

Dividing tasks into small sub-tasks will help you see the task easier and will motivate and relax you. And for that, make a list of Tasks and subtasks so you will organize everything and feel that you are moving forward.

5. Meditate 1 Minute

This technique is very powerful. Sit in a comfortable place, then drink a glass of water, then close your eyes, take three deep breaths and then for 1 minute or more visualize yourself doing a task that you did at some point in your life, which cost you a lot to accomplish and that thanks You got it to your work and effort. Feel the joy, the satisfaction, the pride you felt. And then open your eyes and continue your work.

6. Add Relaxing Music

At the 1-minute meditation council, add relaxing music. I'm not talking about romantic music, or pop or heavy metal. Music that your goal is to free yourself from tensions. You already know that in the course of the Law of Attraction of Success, you have to download relaxing music for these moments. You can also use classical music to give it this effect.

7. Eliminate distractions

This is perhaps the greatest source of current laziness. Distractions such as Facebook, WhatsApp, internet, television or music. Whatever the distraction, eliminate it! Make sure that once you have started with a task you can not be easily distracted

Each time you overcome your laziness and succeed in accomplishing a task, reward yourself. With this, your mind will associate work with reward and you will anchor this in your mind. And so the next few times it will be easier to eliminate laziness. You have realized that everything depends on what you think of yourself and the world around you. That battles are won and lost in our mind. Begin to train your mind with the course of the law of attraction of success, where I will teach you in practical video tutorials the way of thinking and acting to attract prosperity and abundance to your life. Start thinking like a successful person.

Strategies to overcome laziness

Call it what you want: laziness, laziness, demotivation, idleness ... Maybe your problem is not this, but sometimes you are so overwhelmed and overloaded that the scenario paralyzes you. However, in the end, whatever it may be, the result is always the same: immobility before the pending tasks and inability to overcome laziness. The result of not doing what we have to do or doing it with reluctance has direct consequences on our quality of life. In addition, the feeling of guilt for not being able to overcome laziness affects our self-esteem. We all know this sensation in many meanings, although we do not always know how to identify them well and we group them all in the same bag. In the end, the strategies to overcome the situation are the same, regardless of what is behind. Overcoming laziness is much easier than it may seem. You just have to make the decision to do it and implement some simple strategies.

The following strategies will serve you in any situation. Start here to get quick practical results. The advantage of what you are going to see next is that you do not have to start thinking too much, so you can mechanize the system for all those moments where you need to get something quickly.

1. Analyze your environment, are you around more lazy people?

Therefore, consider if there are any people or people around you who have instilled in you that attitude.

Sometimes, our family, friends or partner project us that same discouragement or apathy at the time of starting an activity. Keep it in mind and value it ...

2. Simple things first

As obvious as it seems, it is necessary to remember that to do something you have to start doing it. Thinking about doing it is not worth it, we must execute it, we must initiate the action. The problem is the blockade that accompanies laziness: where do I start? Do not complicate your life and start with the simplest. And if everything is the same, simplify your choice by doing the first thing that comes up. It is not the best way to organize, but it is the most effective way to start doing something.

3. Step by step

Another of the big problems that block us and make us enter lazily is that the tasks are so big that overwhelm us. To get out of there, it's best to divide the tasks into other, smaller tasks to reduce the pressure and stay motivated. This requires thinking a little about what needs to be done, but it is not so bad. Divide the task first in 3, 4 or 5 parts (the ones you need, but not many). If this is still overwhelming, take the first part and divide it again, leaving the others for when it is your turn. If it's still a lot, divide again until you can start with something digestible and have references to move forward. The ideal to obtain good results would be to divide everything into small parts and plan their development. This in itself can be an overwhelming task. But we are talking about overcoming laziness, not about achieving maximum productivity and efficiency, so this is what we need at the moment.

4. Make a to-do list

Sometimes we find ourselves in chaotic situations with a lot of work pending. It is very difficult not to lose track of all the work that needs to be done. How to start with the simplest if you do not know what to do? And to go step by step or talk, because each task is independent. To solve this, sit down for a moment and write down what you have to do in a list in the format you like the most: write everything on paper or in independent notes that you will place on a board, for example. Give yourself this moment to define what you have ahead.

With this list in front, you can already decide. Eliminate superfluous tasks and leave less urgent tasks for another day. Then, take the simplest task, the one that takes the least amount of time and takes that first step.

Then, step by step, move forward in the list. Do not judge yourself, do not try to comprehend intellectually the whole problem. Simply, move forward, crossing out or removing what is done

5. Visualize the benefits of a task done

If you are too lazy to do something because of the effort involved, think about what will happen when it is done. Visualize the result and enjoy it. This will fill you with energy and restore your motivation. Visualizing the finished tasks helps to overcome the inner resistance that was preventing you from getting involved with those tasks. The visualization also helps to pose options on how to solve possible problems to perform a task or to pose something as simple as where to start.

6. Eliminate distractions

Usually, distractions are the source of laziness and the only reason why we decided to postpone tasks for another time, which makes it seem even more boring. Whatever it is that distracts you, eliminate it. Make sure that once you have started one of the tasks there is nothing to distract you. You know very well what it is, for this you will not have to do a great exercise of self-exploration. To conclude, these strategies can be as useful as they are decisive. Sometimes, a small change in our routine is enough to generate changes as positive as productive. Put them into practice.

CHAPTER TWO

How To Get Motivated and Stay Motivated

"Most people ask for happiness on condition. Happiness can only be felt if you don't set any condition."

1 **) Practice patience, perseverance, and prayer**. There's a story of the person who prayed, "God, please give me patience, and hurry!" In this day and age of cell phones, fax machines, and instant gratification, it's easy to want what we want NOW. No one is willing to wait anymore. However, as we mature, we discover that it often takes patience, perseverance, and a lot of hard work to get the things we really want. Whether it's a promotion at work, losing weight, or having a great relationship. If you believe in God, pray for patience, persistence, and guidance. God sees the big picture. We don't. Often, looking back, we see that many of the things we just "had to have" weren't really right for us anyway.

2) Learning how to overcome procrastination helps you get motivated and stay motivated. I believe deep down most people know what they're supposed to do to improve their lives. But we procrastinate doing that activity. We just don't want to do it. Whether it's getting rid of the clutter in our home or office, cleaning up our eating habits or cleaning out the garage. Most of us know there's something we need to do that we've been procrastinating. Yet, by procrastinating a task, we end up cluttering our minds further by thinking about what we should be doing.

Again, if you have certain spiritual beliefs, just ask for the courage to do it. Turn to God. By admitting your weakness you will often gain strength in overcoming procrastination. And getting help in many other areas of your life as well.

Stop trying to do it all yourself. Give yourself a break. Give up some of the control. Take it in baby steps. For example, clean up just half of the garage. Or, begin that exercise program just three days a week for 30 minutes a day. Too often we fall into the "all or nothing" mentality. If we can't do it all at once, well, we simply don't do it at all!

3) Practice positive thinking. Think about what you're thinking about! We often read on the internet that the number one thing people would like to change for the new year is to have a more positive attitude. Thoughts lead to words. Words lead to actions, and your actions determine your approach to your career, relationships, health and just about everything else. Positive thinking is something you often have to practice.

Worry doesn't solve anything. It doesn't add a single day to your life. I make a conscious effort to think about what I'm thinking about. I shift my thinking to the positive whenever possible and it's becoming more of a habit. Becoming more aware of your thoughts is half the battle.

4) Eat right in order to feel happier, healthier, and stay motivated. We all know what to eat but often need to be reminded. Too many junky foods produce junky negative thoughts. Start your morning with protein to stabilize your blood sugar. Increase your daily intake of fresh fruits and vegetables.

Switch to organics whenever possible to avoid exposure to harmful pesticides. If you travel a lot this isn't always easy. Do the best you can. Remember, moderation is the key. The minute you have that all or nothing approach, you set yourself up for disaster by beating yourself up for not being perfect.

See your doctor to find out what types of vitamins and minerals you should be taking. Studies show that even when we're eating at our healthiest many of us are still missing vital nutrients. Drink more water. If you're under a time crunch, and who isn't these days, try eating raw nuts such as almonds or pumpkin seeds for protein and iron. Dried fruits such as apricots, raisins, and cranberries contain vital nutrients and add lots of flavors. I do this all the time when I'm conducting day-long speaking engagements. It's vital for me in keeping up my energy and blood sugar levels not to mention improved mental acuity. Find out what works for you because everyone is different.

5) Make a decision that you will be happy in spite of your circumstances. Don't wait until everything is going your way in order to be content. Otherwise, you will spend much of your life discontented. Avoid the "when script." For example, "When I get that promotion then I'll be happy." Or, "When I get pregnant and have children then I'll be happy." How many times have you heard people say, "Once the kids are grown and out of the house THEN I'll be happy!"

There's always that elusive "when the script" projecting into the future. And just because you count on something positive to happen, docsn't mean it always does. People aren't perfect and can disappoint you. You can lose your job. Your money can disappear. Things won't always go your way. It's okay to plan ahead and set goals for where you want to be. Just make certain you're also happy where you are now.

6) Don't compare yourself to others. We tend to compare the worst in ourselves with the best in others. Don't compare your insides to someone else's outsides. This is especially true for women. In our society, we're bombarded with magazines and media projecting an unrealistic standard of what we are supposed to look like. Many magazines feature ads with supermodels who are six feet tall. Even worse, the photos have been airbrushed and retouched dozens of times. Focus on developing your own unique gifts and talents. If you're too focused on trying to be like other people, you will become discouraged, give up, and lose sight of your dream.

7) Rest, relax, and recharge completely. It's one thing to get motivated, but to stay motivated you need downtime. If you're sleepy on a weekend afternoon, take a nap. In our fast-paced American society, this is virtually impossible during the work week. America is one of the few countries in the world that doesn't take an afternoon break. Lots of scientific research has shown that lack of sleep negatively affects mood, stress levels, mental acuity, weight, and overall performance. If you're tired, you're more likely to snap. You won't be a pleasant person to be around.

8) Exercise plays an important role in getting and staying motivated. For example, many participants in my speaking engagements tell me that walking outdoors during a short lunch break is enough to reenergize them. Exercising outdoors is especially beneficial in helping reduce depression during the winter months.

While you're exercising, and driving to and from work, listen to your favorite music. One of my favorite songs is "It's On," from Boney James "Pure" CD. Very upbeat music with lots of saxophones, and serves as a huge energy booster and mood lifter for me! I'll often play it after finishing a project. It's a small but very positive reward.

9) Get out of yourself. Be grateful for what you have. Do you have enough clothing, food, and a roof over your head? Probably so. Do volunteer work, or spend time listening to a friend or family member in need. By helping others you realize that whatever your "trauma of the day" happens to be, really isn't so important after all.

Ways to self-motivaton when you're discouraged

An essential element to work with more efficiency is self-motivation. However, several unexpected situations in our daily life can discourage us in some moments. It is very common that at times we do not feel like studying, working or doing physical activity, for example. In addition, many people leave everything for later and, in the end, do not reach any of their goals.

Therefore, without doubt, it is very important to know how to become self-motivated. Having control of our thoughts and knowing what to do when we are discouraged can help us improve several situations.

Regardless of external factors, it is necessary to learn to be stimulated so that the results are as positive as possible. We know that the professional path can be turbulent many times. But no one can give up before the first stones he finds in his path.

Here we show you 10 tips to develop your self-motivation and, at the end of this post, you will know how not to give up when you are discouraged.

1. Determine your goals

Many times we can feel unmotivated by not understanding well where we want to go.

The following questions can help you:

- Do you know the reason for doing what you have been doing so far every day?
- What do you want to achieve with the initiatives you take in your day today?
- Why do you want to achieve those goals?

Stopping and questioning about your desires is a way to get to know you better. And having well-defined objectives is a way of self-motivation because when we know well where we want to go, it is much easier to take the necessary attitudes to reach our goals. But be careful not to set goals that are beyond your capacity. Demotivation can be the result of overestimating our strengths. When we are not aware of the magnitude of any situation, we create unnecessary stress in our lives. Therefore, choose your goals conscious of your strengths and the resources you can use. Actually, do you know how to motivate yourself with your goals? Convincing yourself of your main goals and not accepting what is mediocre and comfortable is fantastic to understand what you want to achieve. In addition, it establishes short, medium and long term plans that can be fulfilled.

Plan your goals by listing a list of actions you can do and always mark the items already completed. In that way, you will feel that each time you fulfill one of the actions you live a feeling of self-realization and competence.

2. Change the focus of your thinking

One of the ways to learn how to become self-motivated is to change the focus of your thoughts. Have you ever noticed how we are constantly thinking about what others believe? Or do we even suppose what other people imagine? There are many measures that we take not because we like it, but because we believe they are important to someone. And that may be one of the great reasons for the lack of encouragement. Our suggestion is that you move the focus a bit away from the market and others and that you understand how you feel about everything. Do not try to do the best thinking only of what is external to you. Of course, you need to keep in mind the people around you. But try to do it by understanding how you feel about everything that is around you, and if you realize that it is not what you like, do not be afraid to change. Change is our third item on how to self-motivate when you are discouraged.

3. Make new choices whenever necessary

Sometimes some changes are all we need to encourage us more. And we are not talking about big changes here. They can happen, of course. But you may need only a small modification in what you already do. The new and the unknown always generate a little distrust and even fear. But if you do not try, you will never know if it could have worked. It's not because you spent a lot of time qualifying for a certain task that you need to spend the rest of your life doing that. For example, many people choose to work in niches that they think are the ones they like. Thus, they are constantly dedicated to learning more about their audience and area of action. But, just as we change throughout life, it may be that that person changes his mind about the previously chosen niche. And that's where the lack of courage begins.

For having spent a lot of time studying and doing their best in that area, many do not have the courage to change, because they believe that trying something new from scratch is a step backward. But they can not perceive that insisting on something we do not like more only increases our frustrations. It is necessary to think that the fact of having started in a field of activity does not mean that it is ideal for you. Life is made of choices, and you always have the option to change to something that you like more.

Even if you have dedicated a lot of time to something that you will not do anymore, what you did will not be wasted. Everything we learn can serve to add and help us with something new in the future. Knowing how to achieve self-motivation is also learning that you may want to change your actions, mainly in the professional field. But be careful with indecision. We often deceive ourselves and abandon everything very quickly. The change can be important, yes, but constantly changing without persisting in what you have stated before is not a good strategy. After all, it is necessary to try and make as much effort as possible before making changes. Then, reflect if you are changing to improve or if you are only giving up on something that seems to be very difficult.

4. Do not be afraid of making mistakes

All the good results that we obtained in our professional (and personal) lives occurred because of our plans and executions. This means that achieving your goals does not depend exclusively on luck. Knowing how to motivate yourself is to have the desire to improve yourself, take calculated risks, celebrate victories and mainly learn from your mistakes. Even, to err eventually is healthy, because it is how we manage to discover other ways of doing our tasks in an even better way. Then, learn with your mistakes and accept them! Do not self-punish yourself when you have some stumbling. On the contrary, use it to readjust what you have done, and not to demotivate you. And as an exercise to not make the same mistakes again, you can devote more to studies, which leads to the fifth way of automotive!

5. Learn something new every day

Will and initiative are two essential characteristics of self-motivation. You have to cheer up again and try to change when you're thinking about giving up! Learning something new every day is a great tool for how to become self-motivated whenever necessary. The more information and knowledge we have of a certain issue, the more authority and self-confidence we acquire. This makes us truly believe in our potentials and in what we are doing. Bet on yourself and above all on your knowledge! It establishes educational objectives and tries to achieve them through a lot of study and exchange of information.

If you learn something new every day, you will be more prepared for the possible problems you may face. Do not let the ship capsize and use learning to always self-motivated you.

6. Be positive

Have you heard about the theory that good thoughts generate good results? It is true! Get rid of ideas that may be self-destructive or isolate you. Do not overload your mind with negative thoughts that only discourage you. Of course, it is not easy to always think positively. But there are some steps that can help you when you are out of your mind:

- Search your strengths
- Repeat positive information for yourself. For example: "I can", "I get it", "that's possible".
- Stay in touch with the people who encourage you and avoid those who focus only on your mistakes.
- Believe in your ability to exercise the activities that are your responsibility.
- If necessary, find a specialist to talk and help you find your strengths.

Seeing the world and mainly your attitudes from a positive view help you maintain high energy and motivation.

7. Invest in different sources of satisfaction

It is very important to disconnect from professional tasks at some time of the day. One of the reasons why many people get discouraged is because of not having time for them outside the professional area. And that may be more difficult for those who work at home. Define some timetables for your rest, regardless of where you work.

When you are not involved in situations of your professional life, try to rest your mind and, for this, there are several options for distraction, namely.

- Listen to stimulating music;
- Read books of varied styles;
- Go to the theater;

- Watch movies;
- Travel, even to a place nearby and only for a weekend;
- Do sport;
- To meditate;
- Meet with friends to talk.

Even when there are problems at work, these are the ways to self-motivate not to discourage. With some steps like these, you manage to renew your energies and increase your will to remain firm, strong and motivated.

8. Use coaching tools

Do you know what coaching is? It is a technique that provides people with the tools for their improvement as individuals and, from that, allows them to transform and evolve. Therefore, coaching can help you find your potential. Knowing yourself better allows you to define actions and be able to act towards your objectives. And that is a self-motivation. Then, if you need it, look for coaching help so you can find a reason that makes you move forward.

9. Meet successful people

Have you ever observed how exciting it is to converse with people who achieved their goals? It is very important to have good references, especially if you are starting a new project. Knowing and relating to people who have obtained positive results are good ways to become self-motivated. Everyone has a different story, after all, our results depend a lot on our efforts. However, having contact with someone who has conquered what he wanted can make us study and try harder. In addition, and as we said before, it is very good to have around you people with positive thoughts and who are willing to support you.

10. Get out of your comfort zone

It is very common to get trapped in a comfort zone and be afraid to do things in a different way. However, it is very important to overcome the challenges to achieve your goals (as difficult as it may seem!). Let's suppose that your main objective is to learn English and your biggest difficulty is that you are too embarrassed to speak in front of other people. Although it is not easy, you should take some attitudes that will help you to lose that fear, such as participating in collective conversation classes or talking with people from other countries in online chats, for example. Doing something that costs you can help you a lot in self-motivation, because every time you do something that seemed difficult to you, you will feel happy and more willing to continue working to achieve your goals. Of course, remember what we said above: do not be afraid to make mistakes. If you want to know how to get out of your comfort zone, see our 11 tips on the subject.

11. The day starts well

This tip may seem obvious, but it is very common that when we start badly the day we lower the levels of self-motivation. There is nothing worse than getting up in a bad mood, losing a bus or going to work hungry, right? Therefore, a good way to be more motivated to perform your daily activities and achieve all your goals is to start the day well. Get up early, have a good breakfast and do everything that can help you feel good: do some physical activity, bathe, read a newspaper, listen to your favorite music ... Everything that allows you to have more energy and satisfaction!

12. Date prizes

The last tip to have self-motivation is to give you rewards whenever you reach small goals that help you achieve your great goal. For example, if you do not know how to feel like studying, you can set some challenges, such as reading 30 pages of your material per day. Each week that you meet the challenge you can give yourself a prize, like making a special trip, buying some clothes or watching a movie.Be creative!

CHAPTER THREE

Time Management Secrets of Millionaires

There is no doubt that there are certain things that the rich and the famous implement that the rest of the population is clueless about. There are what we call millionaire habits that translate into profits as opposed to other habits that lead to debt and poverty. One of these habits is sound time management. Without this, there can be no success. Everyone has the same 24 hours and the difference between those that are famous and those that are not is what they do with this 24 hours. Let us see what the millionaires do.

Avoid clutter

Many millionaires have clean desks while their counterparts have desks that look like a tornado just went through them. A clean respectable workspace is a sign of order and organization. This means that trash gets taken out and only that which is necessary for that very minute is retained. The rest is filed away. Clutter reduced the time tasks are accomplished because it takes more time to weed your way through the mess. Millionaire habit number one is-avoid clutter.

Create a task list

Most millionaires create a task list the night before. This is not done on the same morning that the tasks are being done but is situated at the same time they set the alarm for the next day. Some people call this, the Master List. It is a list of 5-10 major items that you intend to tackle for the next day. This makes millionaires "hit the ground running" when morning comes while the rest of the world scrambles to find out what the day holds. By the time they figure this out, the millionaire is far ahead. Millionaires also use automated tools such as software as opposed to notepads.

Time blocks

Millionaires also have a habit of sectioning off a block of time to accomplish the most important tasks. This time block can be anywhere between 45 minutes to 1 hour. During this time, the millionaire does not pick any calls, go to the kitchen or even restroom and does not even look at his email. On the other side, the rest of the population is open to whatever distractions come; from phone calls to spending hours reading and replying to unnecessary emails, to trips to the bathroom and the kitchen. The millionaire, therefore, has a higher degree of concentration and focus when it comes to completing tasks as opposed to the rest of the population which is plagued by complacency and procrastination.

Outsource

Millionaires also do not strive to do all the work themselves. They leverage time and have what is called "SUPER-

PRODUCTIVE TIME". This is the time that they have employed others to make money for them by undertaking highly productive tasks on their behalf. The millionaire also realizes that he or she is not good at everything and gladly and strategically outsources those other tasks to others who have a better handle of them.

Time Management Tools And Techniques

The relationship that the human being establishes with time is complex since a person may not take advantage of the full potential of the current moment by not being focused on what is happening now. This happens when your object of attention focuses on a past memory or, on the contrary, when the rush of anticipation continues leads the protagonist to focus on what he will do when he finishes what he is doing right now. It is vital to organize and manage the time to make the most of the hours, optimize time and be more productive

Time management tools

If you want to improve time management and make better use of your hours, you will ask yourself what resources you have to optimize the minutes. Below, we show 5 time management tools:

1. Agenda

This is one of the most used means of time management and is present in both paper and electronic formats. Choose the option that helps you the most to structure your weekly schedule of tasks and projects.

2. Table calendar

This type of format is practical to have this visual anchoring of the temporary context present in the desk of the work office. For example, you can consult it immediately if you receive a phone call to arrange a meeting. Properly organize tasks and make effective time management, helps prevent work stress.

3. Schedule

Time management seems more complex when it comes to measuring time in a realistic way in the fulfillment of a long-term project. This planning of a script of the tasks that make up this challenge can help you visualize the process to follow from now on.

4. Time management courses

Training around this competence is also present in those training programs with a content linked to this learning objective. The participation in a training experience of these characteristics can help the person to realize what their successes are and what their errors are in the management of the minutes. This learning resource is one of the most important to acquire new skills and abilities in time management.

5. Online resources

Through the new technologies, you can also have digital media-oriented for this purpose. Some online resources that you can use as time management tools are Todoist, Google Calendar, Evernote and MyMemorizer.

- Todoist is a time management tool that allows you to have an updated follow-up of your projects, identifying what you have to do on this day and being able to cross out those points that you have already completed.
- Google Calendar is another of the support resources that can accompany you in this process of organizing your calendar and managing the time better.
- Evernote is another time management tool that helps you constantly keep track of your goals and timeframes.
- MyMemorizer is another time management resource that helps you remember important data through its calendar format that helps you to schedule your tasks.

Time management techniques

How can you optimize your time by improving your productivity at work? In addition to the tools of time management, that is, tools that help to organize, there are also time management techniques: methods that you can follow to make the most of the hours. Next, we show 8 time management techniques:

- **Group similar tasks** to perform them in the same fragment of time to avoid the constant break of rhythm that produces the transition from one issue to another totally different.
- **Specify the tasks in your agenda indicating the start and end time**. This example can be applied, for example, to the convening of work meetings. As important as the

punctuality at the beginning of a job is to finish also in the expected time.

- **Avoid interruptions**. One idea is to place an informative sign on the door of your office in those moments of maximum concentration in which you want to avoid any type of interruption so that the interlocutor knows that this is not a good time to knock on the door.

- **Avoid distractions.** Silence the mobile phone when you can do it to avoid the constant distraction of the news you receive. The provision for the improvement of time management is also part of the planning.

- **Make a weekly or daily list with the list of tasks to be carried out.** In this technique of time management, it is important to differentiate the objectives of this list in order of importance and urgency.

- **Take advantage of the displacements**. To optimize time management in the performance of different errands, you can also perform these tasks in the neighborhood where you live or in the environment close to the workplace.

- **Choose the most appropriate channel in communication to transmit information to another person.** For example, how many conversations of WhatsApp are prolonged in a sequence of messages when that subject could have been clarified better and in shorter brevity through a telephone call?

- **SWOT analysis of time management.** To delve into this objective, you can also carry out this analysis by differentiating four sections of weaknesses, threats, strengths, and opportunities around which you can structure the information. What are the weaknesses that you identify in your time management? And the strengths that you want to continue maintaining? What threats do you identify in relation to this objective? And what are the opportunities present in this scenario?

Time management: tips

In addition to the techniques and time management tools explained above, some tips should also be considered. The 6 most important tips to improve time management are the following:

- Do not postpone what you can do today for another time. Deal with this issue in this day will help you not to accumulate this responsibility for the next day.
- Disconnect from work during the weekend or at the end of the day. Prolonging the day at home until Monday through Friday negatively affects productivity because rest is a basic necessity and lack of sleep affects our brain.
- It poses clear and realistic objectives. The planning connects with an address to follow that is the one that identifies the point of arrival. You may experience disorientation if you do not clearly know where you are going.
- Be realistic and keep a real vision of your time. Wanting to cover more projects than you can really take on a certain period will only make you feel overwhelmed by the feeling of not being able to finish them on the scheduled date.
- Take into account your state and organize the tasks according to him. Through self-knowledge, you can identify, for example, when you have better conditions to

be more productive. It is also better to perform the most difficult tasks in the initial stage of the workday, instead of leaving that effort to the end when fatigue has an effect on concentration.

- Leaves room for contingencies. It is very important to manage time, plan and be specific with tasks, hours and dates. However, it is also important to be flexible and take into account that unforeseen events may occur.

Managing your time, finding balance, and living a complete and joyous life in this day and age almost feels like an oxymoron. Today, more than ever before, we run from one task to another, often times combining tasks just to keep up. If you are running your own business, then the day-to-day tasks are difficult to manage and even more difficult to escape. You're likely thinking about and managing your business 24/7. Coupled with the standard everyday tasks, it may seem like an impossible task to manage your time effectively.

The Effects of Poor Time Management

One of the biggest effects of poor time management is stress. Not the kind of stress that is easily recognizable, but a more pervasive and insidious type of stress. It sneaks in under the radar and causes long-term damage to your health and your overall happiness. Chronic stress, stress that is the result of long term and pervasive stress, causes significant health problems. Chronic stress can be the result of a host of irritating hassles or a long-term life condition, such as a difficult job situation. In people who have higher levels of chronic stress, the stress response lasts longer. Over time, chronic stress can have an effect on:

- The immune system.
- Cardiovascular disease.
- Muscle pain.
- Stomach and intestinal problems.
- Reproductive organs.
- The lungs.
- Skin problems.
- It also causes mental coping issues to arise.

Each of these health issues adds up and cause other issues like diabetes, obesity, heart attacks, chronic fatigue, insomnia and so on.

To put it mildly, chronic stress caused by poor time management can shorten your life and significantly detract from your overall quality of life. It's been estimated that as many as 90% of doctor's visits are for symptoms that are at least partially stress-related.

How Chronic Stress and Poor Time Management Affects Your Business and Your Life

With too many tasks on your plate, it's difficult to focus on any one and prioritizing often seems impossible when everything needs to get done. The result is a tremendous amount of wasted time, not achieving goals, and losing money.

- Loss of control. Poor time management means things will slip through the cracks. When this happens, unfortunately, your customers often pay the price. This causes almost a vicious circle of you trying to appease dissatisfied customers, which then sets you back and adds even more tasks to your list, which again causes more things to slip through the cracks.

- Burnout. Presumably, you started your business, or are starting a business, not only to make money but also to gain personal satisfaction and to spend your days doing something you are interested in and maybe even passionate about. However, even the most desirable activities can become tiresome when you're doing them 80+ hours a week.
- When you manage your time effectively, it gives you the power to set your business aside, for a day, for a week, or even for months, to live the life you want to live and to stay fresh. It's a great way to live and a great way to do business. Imagine your productivity, ingenuity, and enthusiasm if you wake up each and every day excited about the day and what you're going to accomplish.
- No joy. When you spend your days struggling to get it all done, you don't save time for yourself. You don't save time for hobbies, friends, family, and fun. These are the most important things in life and to do without them is to do a great disservice to yourself - especially when it's not necessary. With a little organization and a few tried and true time management practices and tools, you can have your cake and eat it too. You can own and operate a successful business and have time to enjoy life.

What Happens When Entrepreneurs Don't Effectively Manage Their Time?

To be successful, it is important to be able to manage your time effectively. Time management means not allowing distractions. When you don't manage your time effectively:

- Work suffers. Lack of effective time management means hours and hours spent on tasks that are not important leaving only a little bit of time for the projects that really do affect your bottom line. Email or social networking is a prime example. It's too easy to spend an entire morning Twittering, updating your Facebook or linked in page or answering emails.
- Lack of effective time management results also means trying to handle too many tasks at once. Multitasking may seem like a good idea, however, tasks are accomplished much faster when they're dealt with one at a time. Juggle too much at once and a ball is bound to drop from time to time. Unfortunately, the ball you drop may be the most important one.
- Personal life suffers. What do you do if something doesn't get accomplished during normal work hours? Do you work on it in the evenings or on weekends when you could be spending time with your friends and family? Does stress from your business overlap into your daily life making you easy to anger, too tired to socialize and generally unhappy?

Okay, we've talked about what poor time management can do to your health and your business, but what about what good time management can do for you?

Benefits of Time Management

Beyond the basic benefits that include getting more accomplished, satisfied customers, and more profits, not to mention more free time, there are a few benefits you may not have considered.

- Peace of mind. Imagine being able to wrap up your day at 5:00 or 4:00, or whenever you determine is the end of your business day, and feel a sense of calm. Not to have to worry about all that you didn't get done and what is waiting for you the next morning. Being able to effectively manage your time will result in an amazing peace of mind. You can start and end each day with a sense of purpose and peace of mind.
- A sense of achievement and satisfaction. There's tremendous joy in accomplishing goals and checking those important tasks off of your list. When you manage your time effectively, you'll be able to give yourself a pat on the back almost daily.
- More energy. Stress and multitasking are tremendous energy drains. When you manage your time effectively you'll get twice as much accomplished in half the time. You'll sleep better and you'll feel better in your work and personal life.
- More fun. Time management frees up time in your day for the important things in life. Not that owning your own business isn't important, it is, however so are hobbies, vacations, time with friends and family, laughter, exercise and the simple things that make life good.
- A feeling of being in control over your life. When you know what you're doing each day, you accomplish it, and when you have a plan where the action is being taken every day, it gives you a tremendous sense of control. This control can and will expand into other areas of your life, too

CHAPTER FOUR

Awareness As The Cure For Procrastination

Have you ever had a project that you just can't start? As the deadline approaches, have you become distracted by a growing mountain of fear?

Why do we get distracted when it makes our work less pleasant and more difficult?

Self-criticism and procrastination

We turn to procrastination as a way out of negative thoughts and feelings of unworthiness. Procrastination is strongly connected with a self-critical state of mind. Quite right; when we procrastinate, we are not necessarily avoiding our work, but only the critical discourse that occurs when we try to face a challenge.

By incorporating these awareness practices into our daily lives, we can cultivate into a compassionate awareness that serves as a perfect antidote to procrastination.

1. Practice of daily meditation

Imagine trying to write on a blackboard every day without erasing yesterday's scribbles. Here's how our mental state looks when we don't clear our minds.

Meditation is not negotiable - no matter how busy we feel or how many projects we have on our plate, we should always take the time for our practice.

A daily meditation practice builds a healthy detachment from negative thoughts, laying a positive foundation for personal growth. When you sit down to meditate, bring your attention to your breath. Don't worry about trying to erase your thoughts. If you have any mental meander, simply call your attention to your breath. Discover other tools to help you meditate with our pillows and meditation videos.

2. Develop a flow

Focusing on your breathing, you experience it in a Vinyasa yoga class You feel the need to distract yourself from the present moment, bring your awareness to your body. Is there any fear or tension in the muscles?

Notice all the places of discomfort and, instead of trying to escape them, name the feelings. A feeling of tension in the upper back. Recognizing your feelings, rather than reacting to them, will allow you to move through your business without being discouraged by fear. Just like in yoga, this state of awareness gives us perseverance to face challenges.

3. Awareness minute

Procrastination is an impulse that requires self-regulation. Genetically, those of us who are particularly wired for impulsiveness and spontaneity are also more likely to procrastinate.

When you recognize the impulse to check out, check in yourself. Anna Black, author of the book "Mindfulness @ Work", suggests taking a stopwatch, a kitchen timer or a smartphone. Set the timer to 60 seconds. Breathe deeply for allotted time, counting your breaths. When your minute has expired, you will know how many breaths you usually take in a minute. In those moments when you feel like escaping, take a conscious minute - it's all you need to back neutral. When you're done, divide your goals into very small and manageable pieces. I will be able to help you achieve your goals without feeling overwhelmed. Integrating these three awareness practices into daily habits is a wonderful way to strengthen one's sense of self. By learning to embrace in peaceful and satisfying ways, you prepare yourself for personal and professional success. Rather than feeling driven by fear, you will embrace your goals with self-acceptance and a pat on the back.

Finding Time For Tomorrow's Deadline

Finding time is a lifesaver when you are running out of it - quickly! You know that project you found out about two weeks ago but have not worked on yet (the one you kept saying that you would get to tomorrow)? Suddenly that deadline is tomorrow!

Things Not to Do:

- DO NOT leave town, change your identity, or purchase a disguise.
- DO NOT keep procrastinating.
- DO NOT panic.
- DO NOT berate yourself.
- DO NOT throw in the towel.

Details may vary from one time to the next, but the basic story remains the same. You have been putting something off, or letting other priorities get in the way of completing a task. That sinking feeling in the pit of your stomach may make you want to disappear, but showing up is the best antidote.

To successfully complete your task, set new patterns in place. Commit to making this project a success, and use tips below as building blocks for better time choices from here on.

Tips to Help You Get the Job Done.

- DO create a boundary.
- DO get your tools together.
- DO define your task.
- DO get started.
- DO keep in mind that DONE is better than perfect!

Create a boundary. Let others know you need undisturbed time until your project is completed. Enlist in their support, if needed. Let the answering machine take your messages. Direct your full attention and energy to the task at hand.

Assemble your tools. What do you need to complete your task? A computer? Papers from work? Coffee? Gather nearby whatever will help you to get the job done.

Define your task. Envision your endpoint, and brainstorm what you need to reach it. What is the most direct route? Let simplicity be your guide. If you get caught up in the details, it's time to translate thought into action.

Get started. This is the top priority. Once you get started, keep going. Do not let doubts or interruptions stop you. You may hit bumps, but keep moving. Give yourself small breaks if you need to, but set a time frame for them and return to your task quickly.

Finish. Remember, your goal is not perfection, it's to get to the end of this task on schedule. Once you have finished, if you have time, you can go back and polish your work. If it helps, think of your finished product as a starting point rather than an endpoint!

The way you spend your time is the way you live your life

Once you have gotten out of that corner you backed yourself into, congratulate yourself! You have learned first-hand how boundaries, focus and mobilizing yourself enables you to meet your deadline. This is just one example of the benefits you will enjoy if you regularly study your time choices to enhance your effectiveness. Become your own hero. Rescue yourself from a life of urgency and avoidance! With practice, you will experience increased success at finding the time.

Save Money and Time by Curing Procrastination

How many money making opportunities have you come across and filed away in your brain to come back to at some point in the future? If you're anything like me, the point in the future never happened. I can think of countless mundane tasks that would have provided hours of productivity if I completed them on time. Let's not talk about the credit card fees, shut off notices, cancellation slips, warning letters, and the dreaded yellow civil summons being handed over by the unforgiving County Sheriff at my front door. These are all products of my grandmother's old adage: "putting off until tomorrow what I should have done three weeks ago."

Is procrastination a sickness or is it a true case of "lazy-itis?" We will never know.

What I have discovered is that a certain level of adrenaline will push you into "by any means necessary mode." "By any means necessary," the money that I spent leisurely last week will resurface and help me reconnect my phone today. "By any means necessary," I will find the time to write this term paper that is due in two days because graduation depends on it. In some ways, you can compare the feeling you get when you're granted a week extension by the phone company or your professor, to a hit. Oh, it feels so good. You run around the room screaming: "Hallelujah!" You profess to yourself: "This is the last time I'm putting myself through this." Before you know it, you're back to the same behavior.

Like most people today, you have probably spent hundreds or thousands of dollars searching answers on the internet. Get-rich-quick schemes, MLM start-up fees, self-help books that you haven't finished, and the list goes on. I have piles of magazines and newsletters that I've circled and highlighted. But the problem lies within. The first step in curing procrastination is to admit that you wait until the last minute, no matter how costly and painful the consequences are, you are guaranteed to make more money and save more time. You cannot find reasons to justify your procrastination. Many proclaim that the act of procrastinating "makes them better" at what they do. This is a smokescreen. There is no substitute for good time management skills. Once you cure your procrastination, you will feel a lot better.

Watch Your Revenue Grow

Procrastination is behavior based on a whole set of assumed negative outcomes, fueled by an inner critic, which preys on our vulnerabilities and insecurities.

Many entrepreneurs unwittingly sabotage their success by procrastinating. The delay launching websites, products, and services, or making decisions about investing in their business for all sorts of reasons - 'the timing is not right', 'the content needs work', 'more research or information is needed', 'what if I fail?'

When you run your own business this is entirely understandable as any negative feedback on the finished outcome, or failure can be seen as a very personal reflection of your ability.

However, money responds to speed. By not taking action fast enough you could be losing potential revenue opportunities.

The most successful entrepreneurs learn and implement a new idea immediately. They will get their product or service to market faster than the competition and adjust, amend or tweak along the way. They know that getting something done, even if not perfect, is good enough.

If you know that procrastination is keeping you stuck and you could kick yourself that someone else got there before you, then now is the time to "Just do it" as Nike would put it!

Here are 5 tips to help you in the words of Martin Luther King "Take the first step in faith. You don't have to see the whole staircase. Just take the first step".

1. Don't overwork any new product or service before launching it. You will just lose energy and momentum and it will show up in the final results. Actively demonstrating the value of your service and product to your clients, with enthusiasm and excitement, is an important first step.

2. Let go of perfection - it doesn't really exist. There will always be room for improvements! By taking action you will soon get feedback on what does and doesn't work. Then you can make changes and amendments from a place of knowledge and experience.

3. Do the tough task first as it does get easier. You can set yourself a time limit, take short breaks and set up mini rewards along the way. Just imagine how good you'll feel when it's done.

4. Be accountable to someone else, whether this is a colleague, friend or coach. Making the commitment to achieve something within a realistic timescale and communicating this in writing or verbally will set your wheels in motion.

5. Don't be afraid to stop a project if it isn't working out. Being in business means from time to time making painful decisions about whether to continue with a piece of work. This can be tough when you may have invested a lot of your own time and money. But if your energy and focus are on something which is going nowhere fast, then you could be using this as an excuse for not putting your attention on what could be a more profitable product or service. When you face up to when and where you are procrastinating, and are prepared to put one foot in front of the other despite your fears, you will feel much more in control. And that's when your business will really start to take off.

Time And Money

Time and money are two precious commodities. They both have some things in common, you can spend both and you can save both. We all know how to spend money and time, like the Steve Miller song says "time keeps on slipping, slipping, slipping into the future." However, we can be good stewards of those two commodities. Spending less money can be as simple as buying things on sale, buying used, buying online (including online auctions) or not buying them at all. You should only buy the things that you need and when you need them. Spending less time on work and more time with family can be accomplished by working smarter not harder.

How do you work smarter you ask...organization! The organization can save you time! When you need something, you know where it is and can find it instantly. Everything should have a place.

Working for a newspaper such as Eagle Newspapers means working with deadlines. Many of you in the marketplace work with deadlines or "time frames", a point in which a task needs to be completed. Meeting deadlines or these "time frames" means prioritizing. To prioritize, only do what is relevant for the task to be accomplished and try not to waste time with what is irrelevant. Moreover, don't procrastinate! It's a good practice to manage your time effectively, and that means staying focused, being self-motivated and not procrastinating. Time management is not always easy. If a deadline or time frame involves multiple tasks, designate a block of time per task and stick to your schedule.

CHAPTER FIVE

Why It Is Bad To Procrastinate

One thing we have in common is a general tendency to want to put things off until the last possible minute. There are some tricks to apply to the issue that can help you overcome this problem and get things done efficiently. Breaking free from the cycle of procrastination starts with you being able to confess that you are one and that you are looking for ways to beat it. Once you admitted that you are a procrastinator, the next thing to do is to look at how it has negatively affected your life. Did you wait too long to propose? Did your friends come over before you cleaned your room? Begin to look at procrastination through the lens of its effect on your life. Don't try and over guilt yourself about everything you missed out on. Instead, take this opportunity to make a stand and promise yourself that you are going to start to do things on time. The hardest part of the process is going to be with the next tip. You need to find a way to motivate yourself to get things done right away. There is no formula or method that can help you. It has to come from inside, and you need to really want and hunger for it. Any of a million tasks that you need to get out of the way are fair game as far as taking things one by one and getting them done. The key here is to do things, not worry about them and put them off. The more things you do, the less you will want to delay getting things done.

Once you start knocking little things out of the way, you will begin to see the freedom and joy of getting things done early. Pat yourself on the back and you should be proud. However, this is a long process and there are still challenges that lie ahead. Dealing with procrastination cannot be managed overnight, and it will take some time and a lot of setback before you are really getting the upper hand. In the meantime, don't be too hard on yourself as you are developing these new habits, and remember that the less you procrastinate, the happier you will feel about yourself and your life.

Unveiling Why Is It Bad to Procrastinate

Why is it bad to Procrastinate? This is the most common question that is posed by all age groups of people? Since, at one point in life, everybody indulges in procrastination. Few people have this problem for prolonged times, and for a few people, this problem arises owing to particular spheres of life. Irrespective of the stimuli, procrastination effects are considered to be negative and frustrating. They are always associated with poor performance, loss of opportunities, time wastage, and overall feeling terrible about oneself. At the time when an individual procrastinates, what happens is less vital tasks occupies the position of more important tasks, thereby eating up space and time which would have been otherwise utilized for performing imperative actions. Perhaps, now it is clear why is it bad to procrastinate? It is very bad for the morale of any individual as well as an unhealthy habit.

Uncovering the Negatives:

By pondering into major reasons for procrastination, it will become easier to understand why procrastination is bad. Majority of people, do not lack the time but the motivation, subsequent to determining how hard, boring and painful the task is the procrastination behavior comes into full swing. A reason such as since it is very chilling outside and hence no exercise for today. A person thinks that performance is well under pressure and so on are considered to be fairly harmless. Although, they are not as innocuous as they sound, since they upshots in postponing an important project or obligation. Finally, such excuses will only preclude people from attaining vital objectives and makes them feel worse than ever. This explains why is it bad to procrastinate? A person might completely lose hope and give up even attempting any task if confronting more and more failures allowing to procrastination. Stress and lack of positive motivation are the most common side effects of procrastination.

Overview:

Majority of the results produced by procrastination are negative and hence, it is suggested for the growth of every individual to simply alter the behavior patterns to eliminate such undesirable penalties. Why is it bad to procrastinate is because it reinforces itself on the individuals and prevents them from integrating good habits. People normally evade from starting any major task by wisely diverting their attention to things other than what needs to be ideally completed. The recognition of such diversions can help an individual cure the problem of procrastination. Awareness is a good place to begin, in order to tackle this problem. College students normally are the biggest propagators of procrastination, they simply hang out during lectures and projects. Majority of college students attend late night parties and then, the next day is not able to remain awake for their exams. Why Is It Bad to Procrastinate? Simply is answered by such students scorecards.

CHAPTER SIX

Why Do People Procrastinate

Why do people procrastinate? It's tempting to write about it later but that's procrastinating! There are 8 reasons why people put things off, often putting their lives on hold as a result. However, first, understand that it's not all bad. There is both positive and negative procrastination.

Positive Procrastination

This is good stuff. It's time spent exploring, pondering, gathering thoughts to gain clarity before taking action or making a decision. It relates to all areas of life; family, study, work and business decisions, and buying decisions, especially major purchases like a car or house. Positive procrastination is totally necessary to avoid potential disaster.

Negative Procrastination

This is the bad stuff. It's the time spent avoiding taking action or making decisions. It is generally characterized by some form of sabotaging behavior that stops you achieving tasks or goals. You may start many things but never get around to finishing or you may not even start at all. Negative procrastination leads to potential disaster.

To understand why you procrastinate, look within and get to know yourself and recognize your patterns for clues to why you put things off. Reflect on your own behaviors to see which of these 8 reasons apply to you.

Reasons Why People Procrastinate

- **FEAR** - Fear of failure and fear of success. Sounds weird but people often fear the responsibility that comes with success more than they fear failure.
- **LACK OF SELF BELIEF** - This is a really big one. It often manifests from deeply ingrained limiting beliefs, negative self-talk, and self-doubt.
- **LACK OF FOCUS** - With no clear plan or routine to follow, it's easy to become distracted with trivial 'busy activities' therefore achieving very little.
- **POOR WORK HABITS**- Many procrastinators are poor organizers and have difficulty prioritizing tasks and managing time.
- **OVERWHELM** -Too many choices, not knowing how or where to start or what to do first, information overload prevents procrastinators from accomplishing anything.
- **YOUR WAY ISN'T BIG ENOUGH** -If your WHY isn't important enough, you'll lack the drive necessary to achieve. Most likely you don't have clarity of purpose in your life so you give up.
- **PERFECTIONIST** - Perfectionists put off completing tasks until they can get it perfect. Since nothing is ever perfect they never get to the finish line.
- **NO ACCOUNTABILITY OR SUPPORT** - When there is no accountability imposed by deadlines or a boss, for example, procrastinators lose momentum and fizzle

out. Equally, if there is not support they revert to typical self-sabotaging behaviors that prevent finishing tasks.

So there you have it. Once you understand why you procrastinate the next step is to find ways to deal with your procrastination and overcome it. Spend some time positively procrastinating to identify you're why then take measures to fix it. If you need help there are some excellent programs and books available specifically designed to beat procrastination once and for all. DO IT! Make a commitment to end procrastination once and for all.

Self Hypnosis to Cure Procrastination

Hypnosis is an extremely powerful psychological method to consciously communicate with your subconscious mind. And that is the part of your mind that you usually have the least influence about, because it does speak another language. And that language is the language of hypnosis.A lot of people still have all kinds of false ideas about hypnosis. They think of the stage hypnosis show where they witnessed someone making a complete fool out of themselves, behaving like a chicken or impersonating a famous celebrity. Or they think of the hypnotist swinging a big watch in front of the hypnotic subject's eyes, making them sleeping and taking control of all their willpower.

The truth is - hypnosis is not some extreme, intensely unusual state of mind. It is rather an everyday experience that all of us have on a regular basis. However, we mostly are not aware of it when it happens, and we almost never utilize it to achieve something that we want. Whenever you are daydreaming, you are almost always in a kind of hypnotic trance state. When you are lost in thought, or deeply immersed in reading a book that captivates you, it's already a hypnotic trance state.

Now, how can you use that trance state to cure procrastination?

Well, first of all, you have to get into that trance state. Simple relaxation exercises can help to induce this state. Use breathing techniques or guided visualization or self-talk to get into a deeply relaxed, calm state of mind. Then use hypnotic suggestions to overcome procrastination. These can be suggestions like: "I am a proactive person who gets things done. I complete the task that I decide to tackle. I'm a go-getter."

However, the problem with self-hypnosis is that there are quite a few details that you have to take care of. For example, you must have the right tone of voice and use the right kind of words - as well as avoiding the wrong words - to make a hypnotic suggestion effective.

It is also extremely important that you avoid the use of negation. For example, never use sentences like: "I don't procrastinate." because your subconscious mind does not process negation. To your subconscious mind, "I don't procrastinate" sounds just like "I procrastinate".

That is why making use of professionally produced self-hypnosis recordings is probably the most effective way to cure procrastination. Just listen to a hypnotic session whenever you feel like you need to get over your procrastination

How To Cure Procrastination Using NLP

What is NLP?

NLP stands for "Neuro-Linguistic Programming" a method designed to help individuals to progress toward excellence. In specific:

Neuro: Something to do with the mind, the peripheral nervous system (or simply the hands and legs of the mind) and its functions (thinking).

Linguistic: The channels of communication that we used to connect with the world outside.

Programming: A structural process or standard operating procedure (SOP) that our mind runs on. (or simply "habits").

In summary, NLP is a study of how humans interact with their environment and it is base on this study that is used to optimize individual toward their own excellence.

How is procrastination related to NLP?

There is so much relation between NLP and the procrastination. First, you need to view procrastination as a byproduct of the mind. What makes procrastination such a pain for many is that it is an age-old habit that over the times forms as part of your SOP in life. As a procrastinator, you have learned to love and function with procrastination ever since you pick up the habit. Habits are functioning SOP that works in the subconscious level of your mind, which means you will do that sequence of the process without you being aware of it. That would dictate you to be reactive rather than responsive, your subconscious mind works really fast when it comes to familiar inputs like mowing the lawn, washing the dishes or bringing the dog out for a walk. The procrastinator's mind would have long labeled such tasks as undesirable and switch on a sequent of procrastination that usually involves finding reasons or excuses not to do them. It may seem complex to carry out the procrastination sequent but the subconscious mind knows exactly how to carry them out in the quickest and painless fashion that is invisible to the conscious mind.

NLP is designed to deals with bad habits like procrastination within the subconscious mind program. In NLP, the process of relearning has to go through 4 stages:

1. Unconscious incompetence - This is where most chronic procrastinators reside in, they are completely unaware of the existence of their procrastinating habit.

2. Conscious incompetence- By the time you start to notice your procrastinating habit and start to read this article to look for a solution to your procrastinating problem, you have progressed to this stage. You know you got a problem but do not know how to solve it.

3. Conscious competence- At this future stage for most aspiring procrastinators, they have found solutions to their problem and have actively working to tackle the problem. However, they still need lots of conscious effort and time to work through their procrastinating problem whenever they pop up in life.

4. Unconscious competence- The conscious mind has completely hand over the task of tackling procrastination over to the subconscious mind. The ex-procrastinator has turned over a completely new leaf and is now a true blue motivator - a powerhouse that is directed toward his/her own goal.

NLP is used specifically to help those to be completely free from procrastination and become the person that is ever motivated toward excellence. However, it is not a magic tablet that you can swallow and become the person you desire tomorrow. You are right, there are lots of hard work and massive action in the right direction and it is NLP that will provide you with the direction toward mastering your own destiny.

Motivation the Cure For Procrastination

This fifteen letters long word has amongst many factors been the worst cause of mediocrity, indolence, and lack of aspiration attributed to a lot of people on our planet.

This longword hinders many people from achieving anything worthwhile in this life. As a result of this setback, they are unable to archive meaningful objectives mainly because they refuse to take action.

They make it a habit to put things they ought to do immediately off, as long as they could hoping to tackle the job or assignment at a more favorable time in the future which of course, we all know never really comes.

So days turn into weeks, and weeks into months, and months into years but the person remains in the grip of this habit. This process continues until this habit forms in stone and becomes difficult to break.

The word gains a stranglehold on the neck of its captive, as it totally saps their will to act on anything meaningful. It then renders them incapable of initiating and completing any project no matter how easy the task may be.

* Motivation enters

At this stage, the need of the captive is for a quick solution that will free the person to enable him or her live a fulfilled life once again.

Because every action that has a beginning, must of necessity have an end, motivation with less number of letters, but with a better sound to the ears comes to the rescue. And all the captive needed to do was to reach out for it in solace, against the total powerlessness they once felt in the vice-like grip of procrastination.

* How does motivation tackle procrastination?

Motivation does this simply by appealing to the emotion of the captive to get him or her interested in a vocation, an assignment, a business proposal, a talent discovery or a hobby, etc.Motivation keeps the captive engaged in this new found love until the captive is totally consumed by this new love.

This sudden development of this new habit by the captive now creates a reawakening of his hitherto dead senses to try and live a purpose driven life.As the captive comes to terms with the reality of its confinement and attempts to shake itself of the yoke of procrastination to wear the mantle of motivation, the death knell of procrastination is rung.

* Passion

Complete commitment and passion for the new way of life come to a peak and the song of freedom reaches a crescendo as passion overruns procrastination. The captive soon announces its arrival on the scene to the world which hitherto never knew or heard about that person.

As motivation fuels passion, the captive regains all lost glory and the person now rules his world, his confidence grows leading to a bold declaration of his independence forever.

* Freedom expressed

The captive now restored, motivated and empowered, launches out in its newfound vocation or assignment declaring liberty, excellence, and freedom at last.Having won this battle the captive becomes a lethal weapon and a spokesperson against cancer called procrastination. A war the freed captive continues to wage in total commitment to excellence and productivity in his new name called, passion.

Effective Ways to Put Off Procrastination With EFT

You imagine what might happen, not will happen. With Emotional Freedom Techniques, you can remove all your fears from doing tasks that you don't want to do. You can get over the boredom and make any task fun. All tasks seem to become manageable when used with EFT. You are not lazy because you put off doing tasks. You think that something bad will happen. It very seldom does.

Help With Your Priorities.

Emotional Freedom Techniques can help you prioritize your to-do list. Do you have so many things going on that you actually don't do anything? You can spend too much time, doing nothing, then beating yourself up over it. Emotional Freedom Techniques can help you eliminate tasks that are unimportant.

Task Overwhelm.

Using Emotional Freedom Techniques you can alleviate task overwhelm. Often when you have set yourself a goal. You stop yourself from achieving that goal because of deep down, you think it is an impossible task. So you don't even start it.

Time Management.

You have too many tasks. You don't know which ones to do 1st, so you end up doing none of them. This puts pressure on you. Get rid of the pressure with EFT.

You Just Don't Want To Do It.

There are some times when you just don't want to do something. By using EFT you can find these out and either does the task or realize that it is not that important and drop it. Thereby releasing some of the stress and tension that you have built up inside of you.

Pressure From Others.

Do you do tasks because somebody else said you have to do them? How does it make you feel? Angry, sad, frustrated. Do you feel worthless? EFT can help you change your own perceptions of you. Therefore, changing how others see you.

You Like The Pressure?

Stress is not healthy for you. Storing stress in your body can make you very ill. With Emotional Freedom Techniques, you can treat the underlying causes of your stress.

CHAPTER SEVEN

The Power of Self Discipline - Why You Haven't Achieved Your Goals

Have you ever wondered how other people seem to achieve more but yet you work just as hard?

Have you ever wondered how others seem to be more successful and you know that you are just as intelligent, just as capable but yet for some reason you aren't doing as well?

There could be one key ingredient that you are missing to achieving your goals. It is an ingredient that is often taken for granted and overlooked because it is so simple and that is "self-discipline".

What is self-discipline?

It is the ability to do what you should do when you should do it whether you feel like it or not.

This is a quality you need to posses while on your journey to reaching your destination. Without it, you will struggle in reaching your goal.

What has been holding you back?

Before you can begin thinking about how to improve your self-discipline, you need to ask yourself what has been holding you back. This will give you a better idea of your thought processes, your beliefs, your behaviors and what action you can take to empower yourself to make positive changes.

So here are some questions I would like you to consider:

- Why aren't you as successful as you would like to be?
- What beliefs do you think have been disempowering you? and
- What behaviors do you think you could improve on?

Here are some other questions to consider?

- Do you make excuses or procrastinate?
- Are unclear and aren't sure of what you really want?
- Do you think you deserve those rewards or are you unconsciously sabotaging your potential to achieve your goals?
- Is there some part of you that believes you aren't capable?

Or maybe all of the above are just excuses. Here is a secret to making that big change in your life... stop making excuses.

You can either have REASONS or you can have resulted! Which one do you choose?

Are you clear on what you want?

Before we start planning on what actions we can take to move in the right direction, we need to be clear on what that direction is, therefore it is imperative that you understand what success means to you. Everyone has their own definition of success and it doesn't make you right or wrong. It is what works for you and is based on your values. Is it about living up to your own expectations, not someone else's?

So here are 4 more questions for you:

- What does it mean for you to be successful? What does it look like?
- Who are your role models when you think of success?
- What characteristics do your role models possess? Or what is it about them that makes them successful?
- What does success mean to you?

Here are some ideas of what my students have told me success means to them:

- Being able to live in your own way doing what you want to do
- Being the person you want to be
- Achieving the goals you set for yourself
- To be happy and settle for what you want and not for any less
- Feeling satisfied and fulfilled
- To reach success, does it mean that everything has to be perfect? No, because success is about growth and progression. It doesn't have to be static - it can change.

What does it take to be a successful person?

Here are some characteristics I believe successful people tend to possess

- they are disciplined
- they manage their time and actions effectively
- long term thinkers and planners
- willing to make sacrifices and delay gratification
- invest in continual learning
- they make a habit of doing what unsuccessful people don't want to do.

Are you capable of adopting these qualities? Of course, you are. You probably already do in the areas you are successful in but need to improve on them in areas you are still working on achieving. For example - maybe your finances are perfect because you save and manage your budget but your weight isn't ideal because you aren't investing time in consistently exercising.

Self-discipline is necessary for success in order not to give in to temptations. And our two greatest temptations are:

- the path of least resistance, and
- the expediency factor.

It is not our fault. We are all human and they are our weaknesses. We need to be disciplined enough to see past that and aim for RESULTS... otherwise, all you have left are REASONS.

The good news is you can achieve almost any goal you set for yourself if you have self-discipline. The even better news is self-discipline can be learned.

If self-discipline is the key to success then the lack of self-discipline is the key to failure.

Why are habits important to achieving success?

Whatever you do becomes a habit and habits can be hard to break.

They say it takes 21 days to create a habit so the trick is to start doing something/one thing, every day, and after 21 days it will feel weird not to do it. It is your job to refuse to act in any other way that is different from the good habit you are trying to create.

What are the results in achieving success?

You may have not thought of this, but what do you think happens when you start doing things that move you closer to achieving your success? What do you think happens to your self-esteem?

When you follow through with what you set out to do - don't you think you strengthen your trust with yourself?

- You will feel better about yourself
- You will feel more confident
- You will have more pride and self-respect
- You will most probably be willing to try more things because you have proven how capable and disciplined

you really are and as an overall result you end up achieving more success!

Sounds like a fair trade to me.

You can apply self-discipline in any area you want including health, work, finances, relationships, family and education.

5 simple steps to help you be more disciplined:

- Decide and be clear about what you want. You must set achievable goals.
- Determine what price you are willing to pay, that is, what habits are you willing to change? It's the bad habits that get in the way of self-discipline. Be specific about what you are going to do differently on a daily basis. Write it down. Also, write down you're "what ifs" if you do stray.
- Plan the day's activities in advance. If you're not used to planning then start simple. The night before, write down five things that you want to accomplish the next day. Then the next day marks them off as you do them - this is basic self-discipline. It's also forming new good habits and tracking progress.
- Resolve to be willing to pay the price. Take action and do it, and
- Finally, reward yourself for self-discipline accomplishments but make sure you chose rewards that help you move forward, not go backward. Eg if you are trying to lose weight, don't make food your reward.

CHAPTER EIGHT

How To Get Organized

D o you ever look at your home or office and say, "This place is so cluttered! I need to get it together, but I feel like everything is so far gone now...nothing can help!"

Do you ever think about your life and say, "I am a lost cause - I am so disorganized. Where would I even begin?"

If you find that you are contemplating getting organized or acknowledging that your life and surroundings could be more organized, then it is a safe bet that your lack of organization is a stressor for you. The underlying stress may take many physical forms - procrastination, anger, anxiety, and depression - just to name a few. The good news: if you are chronically disorganized, then you can alleviate these negative behaviors by organizing your life, your home, or your office.

The following L-E-S-S-O-N-S can help you prioritize, focus, and accomplish your goals...one step at a time!

* List every task you must complete or want to complete.

Grab 2 sheets of paper and a pen. On the 1st sheet, write down whatever comes to mind, no matter how big or how small it is, how long you have wanted to do it, or who wants you to do it.

Pay no mind to priority or importance of each item at this stage. This is your brainstorming session! You are going to weed through the pile in the next two steps.

* Establish priority order for all tasks.

Look at the list you just created in the previous step. Really examine it. What items are most important to your family, your livelihood, or yourself? What must be accomplished quickly? Those should be your top concerns.

Which thing will be the most or the least fun? Which thing will be the most or least stressful? As you begin to create your prioritized list of tasks, order it so that you fluctuate between the better tasks and the worse tasks. This serves as a small motivator; you know that when you are working on a rather unpleasant job, that the upcoming one will not be nearly as bad!

Since you have given the list a little thought, it's time to use the 2nd sheet of paper. Number each line. Choose the most crucial "To Do" of the lot and place it in the #1 position, and then continue through all the numbers until you are finished ranking the tasks.

* Select the most important task of all and start with it.

Your focus should be whatever task made it into the #1 spot on your list. Once you are done with #1, move onto #2.

* Set a time limit to carry out this task.

There are two parts to this step.

- Set a long-term goal, such as "Cleaning out my garage will take me two full weeks." Be realistic when you do this, or else you will be setting yourself up for failure. Give yourself double the time you think it will take you. If you believe a project will take you 4 days, give yourself 8 days. The extra time never hurts! If something comes up and you need the extra time, you will not be stressed out because you are missing the deadline. If you finish early, you can pat yourself on the back for reaching your goal ahead of schedule. The key is to set a deadline and stick to it.

- Divide the long-term goal into smaller chunks, such as "I will work on my garage on Saturday mornings from 8-1130am and Tuesday and Thursday evenings from 8-10pm." Be specific on your days and times, making an appointment with yourself for each period and marking them respectively on your calendar. What's even more important than making the appointment with yourself? Keeping it. Decide that you have the discipline to follow-through; your mentality is half the battle!

* Omit distractions of any kind.

Put the kids to bed. Put the dog outside. Turn off the ringer on the phone. Power down your cell. Turn off the TV. Close the front door and don't answer the doorbell. By eliminating factors that could cause disruptions, you are setting yourself up for success in the next step.

* Never lose focus on the task at hand.

Keep on keeping on. Don't allow yourself unnecessary breaks, as they will deplete your time and energy, and may even divert your attention away from the goal and onto something else completely. Set an alarm to go off when your session will be over and remain attentive until the alarm sounds.

If you find that you are having trouble staying focused, then decrease the time allotted for the smaller sessions. Instead of working for 4 hours, try 3 hours.

* Show yourself some love.

When you complete a goal, you should reward yourself. Get a pedicure, play a round of golf, go shopping - whatever makes you happy and relaxed. And you will enjoy the moment, even more, knowing that you have taken another giant step toward getting organized!

So, let's review the steps...

- List every task.
- Establish priority order.
- Select the most important task and start with it.
- Set a time limit.
- Omit distractions.
- Never lose focus.
- Show yourself some love.

How Important Is Organizing One's Time?

Organizing time will empower you to track your efficiency and at the same time create time for yourself.

Jot down the dates of one week and then write down all those tasks/ time slots which cannot be changed. These are the tasks to be done on those days no matter what. Also, make a note of how you will consume your free time. This will assist you to realize how you spend all the time in a day.

Also, you should be keeping track of your travel times (to and from work). Your household chores to need to be recorded. Any special activities you have to participate in. If you are mindful, make sure you keep track of the time for that. Your

family activities have to be listed because family comes first. You will also have to take into account entertainment and fun. Looking at the data for one week, you can analyze your plans for the future. Try to take down any likely changes that you have made that make your management of time better. Subsequently, analyze the results in about a week or so and take a look at what you should be spending more time on. Look at how you can manage some of the time needed throughout the day.

Are you setting up clear times when beginning projects and ending them? After arranging those projects, you have to make sure you have some extra time to do those unscheduled ones on the list. You must be willing to make some general changes in your life if you want this to work. Make sure you plan everything in your day into the time table. This way you can account for all the time spent, and more importantly, for the time that is wasted.

It's important to organize your life. When everything is more organized you can do and achieve much more. In fact, success depends to a large degree on how well you can organize things. And what would your life look like if it was ideally organized?

Clearly, having an organized life means to capture every worthwhile thought in a way that efficiently facilitates action on all things important to you, without losing out on precious moments of time, giving you the best possible chance of succeeding with whatever you desire.

There are 3 major areas of life in which you will experience the pressures and frustrations of being disorganized or the freedom and flexibility of being well organized.

First, there is the physical realm. This includes people around you, the location you live, the practical things like financial management and your health.

The Emotional Realm organizes your 'spiritual' (whatever that means to you) and emotional experience of life. Your pursuit of happiness and love, tranquility, and adventure.

The third is the mental realm. To mentally organize your thinking. This area involves your mental capacities of learning, questioning, reasoning, etc. All vital to be able to really organize things properly.

We can also break our lifestyle into 3 ranges. The following 3 exercises help you control those 3 ranges whilst improving awareness of the 3 realms.

A. Short Range: 10 Minutes Get-On-Track Exercise. During emotional or mental confusion you can sit for 10 minutes or so and write down what's on your mind. It's so surprising that an exercise as simple as that can significantly help you get organized. In fact, it's one of the very best techniques for organized living and controlling the 3 realms.

B. Medium Range: Weekend Review to Organize Life. On a regular basis, perhaps weekly or so, take some extra time to think through the past week and project ahead into the week coming. Use your calendar when you do this weekend review and you will easily find your life becoming more organized.

A Weekly Review is extremely valuable. It puts a 'sheen of success' over everything you do. Try it for a few weeks and see what difference it makes to how well you organize life.

Quite frankly, it's tough to work to maintain this discipline, until you are emotionally attached to the results it produces. So try your best to make it happen every week. Don't let your brain 'forget' about doing it too often.

Just like the 10-minute review, the weekly review can be done with pen and paper sitting quietly for just a short while to consider the past and new week's activities and schedule.

You could compare the previous week's notes with what you write down at each Weekly Review to see your progress. If you keep this up, you'll be amazed at how things begin to change for you.

C. Long-Range: Your Life's Big Picture. Here's a fact established by Brian Tracy. 3% of the population write down their goals.

See how much you can write down about what's genuinely important to you. Some people go through life never really knowing. Writing these things down will probably produce some aha moments. And will also motivate you strongly to organize your life for what's important to you.

How easily would you agree that the three techniques I've outlined are significant aspects to organize life? Again they are:

1. Regular 10 Minute Get-On-Track Reviews.

2. Weekly Self-Assessment Reviews.

3. Your Life's Big Picture Reviews

Even if you are unclear of all the benefits or you're unsure exactly how to do those 3 techniques, just start. Start from now. Really. I mean don't just read this article, use it. They will genuinely help you organize life.

Assess Your Situation and Improve Your Life

Have you ever asked yourself, "What can I do to improve myself and my life?" Many people have asked themselves this question at some point in their lives as part of their personal development and to help them achieve their goals.

Life is a journey and sometimes we can get stuck in the same position for a long time or we may even get lost. There are times when we may get frustrated by our lack of progress or insufficient progress in our personal or professional lives. This is when we need to stop and take the time to analyze ourselves and our lives. We need to look at where we are in life, where we want to go, and how we intend to get there. One of the best ways to do this is by writing and using a strategic plan for your life.

To write a strategic plan for your life you need to focus on your current situation, values, vision, purpose, mission, dreams, goals, strategy, action plans, and how you will monitor and evaluate your plan and take corrective actions when necessary.In writing a strategic plan, you begin by assessing your current situation or where you are in life right now. Various tools can be used to do this. One of the best tools that can be used to assess your current situation is SWOC, an acronym for strengths, weaknesses, opportunities, and challenges. Strengths and weaknesses are considered internal factors, most of which are within your control. Opportunities and challenges are considered external factors, most of which are outside your control. Your strengths and opportunities are things you can use to help you improve yourself and your life. Your weaknesses and challenges are things you need to improve and manage.

A SWOC helps you see what is happening in your life and how you can make changes to have a better life. Doing SWOC is very easy. Get a sheet of paper and create a 2X2 grid. This will give you four cells, which are to be labeled as Strengths, Weaknesses, Opportunities, and Challenges. You can have any number of things under each heading. Think about yourself and your life, and then under Strengths, list everything you are good at and the significant resources that you have. As you do so, remember that being a part of God and one with God is a phenomenal strength. Your knowledge, talents, and network of family and friends are also strengths.

Under Weaknesses, list your areas for improvement. We all have areas for improvement in ourselves and our lives. If you are not sure what areas you need to improve, you can ask someone who you believe will tell you the truth. Sometimes it is easier to identify areas for improvement in others than it is to identify them for ourselves. You can ask the person to help you identify your strengths as well as your areas for improvement. As you do your SWOC, focus on the major areas for improvement and those that will help you live a better life.

Under Opportunities, list the things you think you can do to improve yourself and your life, your options in life, and things you believe are possible for you. Think about new things you can do, things that can be done differently and better, and keep an open mind.

Under Challenges, list some of the major difficulties you are experiencing, the obstacles you face, and any major threat in your life. As you list your strengths, weaknesses, opportunities, and challenges, also include political issues, economic factors, social issues, technology, legal issues, and environmental issues that affect you.

Think also about your spirituality, health, finances, family, friends, relationships, job, career, business, personal development, love, peace, joy, how much you are truly enjoying your life, and other important aspects.

After identifying your strengths, weakness, opportunities, and challenges, ask yourself the following questions:

- How can I use my strengths to help myself, serve others, and live a better life?
- Which of my weaknesses do I need to improve, and how can I improve them?
- What opportunities can I explore to improve myself and my life?
- What can I do about the challenges I face?

Doing this SWOC analysis will enable you to see various aspects of yourself and your life better so you can improve them.

Benefits of Getting Organized

Save Time - One benefit of getting organized is to save yourself time. Imagine finding everything you're looking for immediately. You know where to go to find it, and it's there. No digging through things, trying to remember where you saw it last, wasting your time, etc. This goes for anything, papers, kitchen utensils, laundry, sporting goods... It applies to your entire life. Give everything in your home a place to belong.

Save Money - Who doesn't want to save money! Getting organized will help you do that in several ways. Having your bills organized properly will ensure they are all paid on time, resulting in no late fees or penalties. Planning ahead for meals will help you save money on food and trips to the grocery store. In turn, it will eliminate the need to order out for dinner at the last second. It will also prevent you from buying duplicate items, not realizing you already had one of something hidden away somewhere you didn't know about.

Reduce Stress - You will no longer have the stress of walking over toys, around piles of laundry or having to locate your bed in order to sleep in it. Getting organized brings order and peace to your life and home instead of chaos. You won't have to run around looking for things, worrying about being late to wherever you're going. You won't forget appointments because you will have a calendar system that works for you. Arguments over lost items will go away.

Increase Productivity - Getting organized also helps you become more efficient in what you're doing. Everything is organized and you're planning meals, shopping on a schedule, paying bills on time, papers are all filed where you can find them, etc. You've found extra time in your day you didn't realize you had. Great! Use that extra time to be more productive and do those things you've always talked about like painting that back bedroom, or taking a cooking class, or spending more time reading... whatever it is you want to do. Being better organized actually creates time for you to do things you prefer to do.

Feel Empowered - Some things you have no control over, but you DO have control over how you manage your home life. Getting your life in order will increase your sense of self-esteem, confidence, and pride. Wouldn't it feel great to open your door to an unexpected guest and not feel like you need to send them away? Instead, you'll feel proud of your home and feel inclined to invite them in without having a panic attack.

CHAPTER NINE

General knowledge on procrastination

Maybe you've experienced being inspired or feeling compelled to take specific action at a specific time, and you found you were right to act on it. And, maybe you've had the same experience I have, where you procrastinate, only to discover you were right to do so. Do you find the first example easier to trust or allow than the second? I'd say many, if not most, people feel like that. We've been taught to be prejudiced in this way.

Trusting your intuitive impulse to procrastinate can be a challenging mental and emotional place to be in, because something inside you is urging you to not take action, yet others are pressing you to do so or you can hear those who talk and teach about taking action chattering in your mind. You may go into self-judgment mode, and that makes you feel even worse. OR, maybe you've learned to trust the particular feeling that happens at those times.

If intuitive procrastination proved to be the right thing to do about a particular matter, that's one thing. What else might be going on when procrastination happens?

When you focus on anything, you summon it to you. The way to summon productively is to create an energy grid; then you must allow the grid to be filled in. Think of this like a house being built. The frame is up and you can see through the grid work of the boards; you have somewhat of an idea what the house will look like. Then walls go up and you begin to get a better image of what it will look like as it gets more and more filled in.

Your grid is your point of attraction. When you create your grid, you want to think and feel deliberately rather than "all over the place," as may often happen with thoughts and feelings. And, despite what you've been told, you do not want to put specifics into the grid; all those specific details will slow the energy and make you work harder than you need to. You want to aim at general feelings with words like ease, comfort, appreciation, confidence, serenity, enthusiasm, joy, love, well-being, worthiness, right place, right time, right people, abundance, means to accomplish, etc., in your grid. This is the framework you create.

Each time you put a general word into your grid, feel what it's like to feel the energy of the word, e.g., what does ease feel like; what does enthusiasm feel like? Let the feelings, not specific details, do the work for you energetically.

Your grid is a reflection of or is constructed by your active beliefs, thoughts, and feelings. Too often, we decide what we want then push ourselves toward what we desire (or believe we're supposed to) rather than allow it to come to us, whether the pushing is mental, emotional, physical, or all three. We tend to leave the spiritual aspect out of the equation; yet, that spiritual energy work is what gets the ball rolling, so to speak, and in our favor, and is what the "allowing" is about (more on this as we go). All that pushing usually or eventually puts us up against an obstruction of some kind, so we push or struggle even more, or we stop in our tracks-we procrastinate, or the Universe procrastinates on our behalf.

Procrastination can come from resistance to doing something you're required to do rather than inspired to do, as you construct your grid of experiences and manifestations. When you feel inspired, you are eager to take action. When you feel required but uninspired to take action, you can feel unenthusiastic, put upon, or resistant.

When you procrastinate about doing something you know you need to do, check the Whys. Why do you need to do it; is there any benefit to you or others, or both, if you take this action? Why do you hesitate about getting started?

If you know you really need to do something and aren't feeling inspired, aren't feeling cooperation from the Universe (or yourself), you might assess the conversation you're having with yourself and the Universe about this thing. Is your conversation creating alignment for you about doing the needed action? If it isn't, you can be certain it isn't creating the alignment with Law of Attraction you truly desire either. So, you want to change your conversation.

Procrastination happens when we try to take action before the energies are aligned. We're trying to move something forward through action rather than moving it forward with aligned momentum. We need to enlist the cooperation of the Universe by doing the energy work first, which is how the grid serves us: we use the grid to align our vibration with the vibration of what we wish to experience.

Releasing disempowering, resistant, worried, anxious thoughts and frenetic activity opens your energy - maybe "relaxes your energy" is a better term to use - so that your vibration can go up. When your vibration goes up, you get closer to the frequency of Source. The frequency of Source is alignment, never strain; if you're straining on any level, you're moving away from alignment. Don't judge that; let it draw your attention to what's happening so you can shift it. You know when you're in alignment or not by how you feel. If you feel good or great feelings, you are aligned; if you have bad feelings, you aren't. The thing to remember is that you can practice your way out of bad feelings by releasing any unwanted thoughts and filling in that space with general thoughts, like those mentioned above, and feeling their vibrations.

Let's get back to procrastination. What are we supposed to do when we bump up against some forms of procrastination? Don't try to push through it. You can't buck that current. Go do something fun. There are times when you might be penalized for doing this. Take this into consideration, but know there are times you need to procrastinate because the Universe IS assisting you; times when you need to procrastinate because you need to pause and align your energy with your desired experience; and times when you procrastinate because you need to recharge your energy at the mental, emotional, and physical levels.

Rushing around with a frenzied energy or having too many things to do makes and keeps our energy vibration low, not high, the way we need it to be for alignment to happen. When we want or want to do too many things at one time, we diffuse our energy and cause a shortage of focus. A low vibration and shortage of focus creates struggle.

That last part about "never did the plowing" might confuse some. When you focus on aligning your energy vibration to the energy vibration of what you choose to experience or create, you are working, but more effortlessly. And, you will also, in that place of alignment, receive inspired ideas. You'll also find people look for you to connect with, rather than you looking for them. Yes, you take action as needed, but you don't need to take more action than is really needed. You act, and you allow the Universe to direct what or who fulfills your desire to you so you connect with it or them, by holding the vibration.

Remember, it's more effective to choose a good feeling and practice feeling it often, until inspired ideas begin to arrive and then you take inspired action you feel eager about. It's more effective to relax and recharge, or revisit your Whys and conversations with yourself and Source when you feel procrastination. It's a good idea to get familiar with the feeling that comes with procrastination you are meant to trust that is operating in your behalf. You are meant to create and enjoy the creative energy grid of your choice. Create a grid for any project, phone call, or whatever you wish to experience. It's a good practice, one you'll appreciate

CONCLUSION

Many people seek the cure for procrastination; however, far too many of those same people think that the cure is as impossible to find as the fountain of youth. Luckily, those people are wrong.

So, first, why do people procrastinate? Well, people waste time generally because of an emotional "secondary benefit". A little more clearly, to procrastinate is to get some emotional benefit from not achieving your goals.

But this means that you haven't delved deeply enough into the problem. Trust me, you're getting something out of it. The most common reasons for procrastination are fear of failure and fear of success. You'll know if you have either of these because the idea of doing the project itself will scare you because the ramifications of trying are either that you might fail horribly or you might get what you want and it'll destroy your life. To rid yourself of this procrastination, you need to focus on what causes you to feel like you're going to fail or hate your success. Why is that the only possible result? What stops you from actually succeeding? (Other than procrastination that is!) The recognition that trying actually offers you the chance of succeeding, and procrastination always only offers failure is usually enough to change this behavior.

But another common set of reasons to procrastinate are overwork, under-appreciation, lack of interest, and general lack of purpose.

If you're overworked, the answer is simple: stop working so much. Either work faster or give up some tasks. The real problem you need to figure out is why do you overwork in the first place. Most people overwork because of a fear of failure--either they take on too many tasks because they fear they'll fail if they don't or they can't say no to projects.

Under-appreciation, you must remember, is in your head. If you're not appreciated, wasting time isn't going to help matters. This is kind of like feeling bad in a relationship and giving up. You need to deal with this issue however is best for you: bring it up with your boss, find a new job, get used to the level of appreciation you get, try to take on more tasks to prove your worth, etc. It really depends on the situation in this case, however.

If you aren't interested in what you're doing, then ask yourself why you're doing it. If you're like me, you can do anything all day every day as long as you're interested in it--and if you're not, you can't do it for any moment any day. In this case, you either need to find or create an interest in the task or find something else to do.

Finally, some people suffer from a general lack of purpose, what we call"alienation". These poor souls just don't really feel like they're connected to anything and feel "angst", that the world just doesn't respond to their wants. Generally, this arises from not being connected to the world around you because you're not doing the things that you want to do. In other words, you're not being yourself. As soon as you dedicate yourself to something you truly desire, this feeling will go away. Though, doing that may be very difficult... a great place to start is to ask what you'd do if you had no limitations...